THEIR
MYSTERIOUS
WAYS

THEIR MYSTERIOUS WAYS

EDITED BY PHYLLIS HOBE

A GUIDEPOSTS BOOK

ACKNOWLEDGMENTS

Every attempt has been made to credit the sources of copyrighted material used in this book. If any such acknowledgment has been inadvertently omitted or miscredited, receipt of such information would be appreciated.

"Go With God, Shadow," by Sally Rosenthal, "A Bird's Message," by Anne Cederberg, and "The Quality of Mercy," by Bianca Rothschild, are from *Angel Animals,* Copyright © 1999, 2007 by Allen and Linda Anderson. Reprinted by permission of New World Library, Novato, CA.

"Holy Cow," by Jody Seay, is from *Animals As Teachers & Healers,* by Susan Chernak McElroy. Copyright © 1996, 1997 by Susan Chernak McElroy. Used by permission of Ballantine Books, a division of Random House, Inc.

"Weela, a Community Hero" is from *It Takes a Dog to Raise a Village,* by Ruth Gordon. Copyright © 2000 Ruth Gordon. Published by Willow Creek Press.

"Kimberly's Best Friend," by Brad Steiger, is from *Cat Caught My Heart,* by Michael Capuzzo and Teresa Banik Capuzzo. Copyright © 1999 by Michael Capuzzo and Teresa Banik Capuzzo. Published by Bantam Books. Used by permission of the author.

"Companion Pieces," by Christine Herman Merrill, is from *Dog People,* edited by Michael J. Rosen. Copyright © 1995 by Michael J. Rosen. Published by Artisan, a Division of Workman Publishing, Inc.

"Caliban," by Henry S. F. Cooper, is from *The Audubon Book of True Nature Stories.* Copyright 1958, Thomas Y. Crowell Co. Published by Thomas Y. Crowell Co., New York.

The following stories are used by permission of the authors:
"Black Magic," "How Jellybean Went to Kansas," "The Man Who Hated Cats" and "The Summer of the Ham Sandwiches," Diane M. Ciarloni; "The Eagle's Answer," Brooke Martini; "The Peacekeeper" and "For Such a Time As This," Gloria Cassity Stargel; "The Bird Woman of Moscow," Linda Holland; "At Peace" and "The Power of Love," Mary M. Alward; "Barney's Gift," "The Bobcat," "Private Smith's Joey" and "A True Friendship," Lynn Seely; "The Renegade Parrots," Lonnie Hull DuPont; "One Last Time," Terri Castillo-Chapin; "A New Beginning," Sara Jordan; "The Lady Wore Black," Thomas Peevey; "Buckwheat, the Singing Dog," and "The Unseen Bird," Mary Alice Baumgardner; "The Gatekeeper," Gayle Trent; "The Lord Works in Mysterious Ways," "Vera and the Mockingbirds" and "The Something That Went Thump in the Night," Renie Szilak Burghardt; "Memorial Services," Joe McCabe; "A Miracle Named Munchie," Thirza Peevey; "The Aquarium in Our Living Room" and "His Reason for Visiting," Ruby Bayan; "The Girls," Barbara Seitz; "Mallard Fever," R. D. Larson; "Golden Star Lost," Garnet Hunt White; "Lonely Lady's Journey," Carolyn Piper; "A Home for Life," Drue Ann Hargis-Ramirez; "Here Comes Charlie," Peggy Williams; "Gone With the Wind-ow," Pamela Sue Coghlan; "The Day the Cows Could Count," Kathryn Mays as told to Lonnie Hull DuPont; "Miracle Dog," Crystal Ward Kent; "Wings of Comfort" and "Catfish Promises," Anne Culbreath Watkins; "The House Blessing," T. J. Banks; "You Knew All Along," Ann Vitale; "That's What Friends Are For," Nancy B. Gibbs; "A Prince of a Dog," Phyllis Hobe; "Remembering Henry," Clyde Gehman; "The Gift That Keeps On Giving" and "One in a Million," Gina Romsdahl; "A Quail of a Story," Art Lienhart; "Robbie's Legacy," Ray McDonald; "The Cat Who Came Back," Carol Wallace; "Tidings of Comfort," Evelyn Bence; "Belated Gifts," Teresa Olive; "Rescuing Baxter," Sue Hersom; "Connections," Dr. Janice K. Wiesen.

Designed by Jerry O'Brien
Illustrations by Ron Bucalo
Cover designed by the Puckett Group
Printed in the United States of America

Contents

v

CHAPTER 6

Finding the Way Home ◆ 133

CHAPTER 7

Comfort in the Hard Times ◆ 159

Introduction

As I work at my desk, I am usually surrounded by two dogs and two cats who seem to take pleasure in being near me even when I am not paying attention to them. They also like to play with me when I'm ready for fun. They enjoy a lot of the things I like to do—reading, being with friends, riding in the car, even if it's a short trip to the post office. When they don't particularly like something, such as my taste in music, they put up with it in the most charitable way.

Since we spend so much time together, my animals know a great many words because I talk to them a lot. But even when I can't find words to express my feelings, they sense what is going on in me and they respond to it. There is no sadness or anxiety that I can hide from them, and they comfort me the moment they detect my need for it. As for celebration, they are the most joyous when I am.

Anyone who has had a close relationship with animals—sometimes even briefly—has wondered how they seem to know so much about us. The answer is profoundly simple: they know our Creator. He sends them to us with His love.

The true stories in THEIR MYSTERIOUS WAYS are about the many blessings God's animals bring to our lives. In our first chapter, *Life-Changing Moments*, we meet animals who help us to confront our adversities and rebuild our lives. Shadow, a stray cat, befriends a woman who is losing her vision and convinces her that she still can make a difference in the world. In "The Peacekeeper," a young Marine learns the value of kindness when he is pursued by several neighborhood dogs.

How often the love of an animal helps us to carry a burden. In *Gifts From God,* a stressed-out couple find peace in a wilderness retreat as they watch some wild creatures and their young. A tiny black-and-white kitten lifts the spirits of a talented musician who is struggling with a serious illness.

Sometimes an animal can help us to make a decision about the direction our lives will take. In *Special Messengers,* a bobcat in a carnival teaches a young girl that freedom also means responsibility. "Buckwheat, the Singing Dog" introduces us to a delightful dog who is happier being with his family than in show business.

Animals often come to our rescue and save us from harm. In *Time of Danger* salutes an incredibly courageous Pit Bull Terrier named Weela for saving scores of people and animals during a devastating flood. And a rooster, of all creatures, guides two women to safety when they are lost in the woods.

In *A Healing Touch,* we learn that the love of an animal can be the medicine that makes us whole again. A woman who is mourning the loss of her son finds spiritual comfort in the song of an unseen bird. We also meet "A Miracle Named Munchie," a gentle pony whose owner has been paralyzed by a rare disease.

Finding the Way Home describes some amazing journeys of animals who refuse to be separated from the people they love. You will be deeply touched by two wild Mallard ducks who are resettled on a distant pond, and try to fly back to the young girl who befriended them. You will also hold your breath in suspense as the owners of a beloved cat discover that he is lost.

In *Comfort in the Hard Times* we meet animals who bring us reassurance in our times of need. A grieving woman is lifted out of her depression by a tiny butterfly that comes close enough to be touched. A large dog with a ball in his mouth brings hope to a grandmother waiting for word about her ailing grandchild.

The stories in *Unexpected Guests* bring us animals who suddenly appear to let us know how much God loves us. Harry, a stray cat, adopts a family that is coming apart and puts them back together again. Caliban, a young grackle who falls out of a nest in Central Park, ends up in a country town where he develops a knack for befriending lonely people.

In our final chapter, *Saying Goodbye,* we discover that when we lose an animal we love, its spirit lives on in our lives. A woman and her son, awakened in the night by sounds of their dog who has died, realize that he has come to tell them he is well. In "Rescuing Baxter," a volunteer foster mom struggles to turn over the kitten she has nurtured when a loving home is found for him.

The special love that brings animals and people together is a reflection of God's love for us. His wonderful creatures tell us that He is always near, and that He cares about each and every moment in our lives. The stories in THEIR MYSTERIOUS WAYS are about the angels He sends to bless us with their ordinary presence, their unconditional love and their dependence upon God's provision for all our needs. And, as I mentioned earlier, all these stories are true.

PHYLLIS HOBE

Life-Changing Moments

Be strong and of a good courage,

fear not, nor be afraid...

(Deuteronomy 31:6, KJV).

"Go With God, Shadow"

SALLY ROSENTHAL

"Of course there are angels," said one of the two clergymen who are frequent commentators on spirituality for the national morning news show I like to watch. "Sometimes," the other cleric added, "even people are really our angels." Looking at Shadow, the ginger tabby who lay sleeping on the sofa beside me, I added, "And animals."

My life had taken a difficult turn when Shadow, a former stray cat, appeared on our patio two years earlier. At the time I met him, I wasn't looking for a fourth cat, or an angel. But I needed one.

I had started losing my vision. This made it necessary for me to leave a career in occupational therapy at a local psychiatric hospital, and I missed my role as nurturer. My resilience ebbed daily. It was hard adjusting to my changing identity and believing in my own worth. I certainly wasn't ready to accept the esoteric idea that angels could help me with the changes I faced.

Around this time of transition, a neighbor reported seeing a stray cat. I decided to set out bowls of food and water. Each morning, the bowls were spotlessly clean, but I hadn't yet seen my elusive visitor. Occasionally, I saw a blur streak through a bush. Is this a shadow or the stray? I wondered. With my vision deteriorating, I couldn't be sure. Then one morning a cat purred and brushed against my legs as I filled the bowls.

When he finally let me see his rough, dirty fur, the timid creature might have been charitably described as "ordinary." But I knew intuitively from our first meeting that this cat was special. He began to appear, as if out of nowhere, when I opened the front door. When he became comfortable around me, he even welcomed gentle stroking. He seemed to sense that I couldn't see him clearly because he always signaled his presence with a meow or physical contact. Then he started the routine of following me when I walked around our condominium complex. And I began to wonder, Who is the real caretaker in this relationship?

This cat seemed to know what I wanted him to do before I mentioned it. If he followed my husband and me to our car, I asked him to return to the lawn and stay safely out of traffic's way. Much to my husband's amazement, the stray cat trotted back to the grass and curled up. I began to suspect that the cat, who now answered to Shadow, had a plan, and that plan included me.

I worried about Shadow when he wasn't around. I didn't think that I could bring a feral cat indoors with three pampered house cats. Each night when Shadow appeared on our patio to say good night, I wondered if he'd be safe and if I'd find him sitting by the bowls the next morning. Then I noticed that Shadow was inspiring even more uncharacteristic behavior in me. I found myself stroking his head each night and saying to him, "Go with God, Shadow."

In the mornings, as he waited patiently for me to fill his bowls, Shadow tried to reassure me that he was hale and hardy with a purr or a thrust of his head into my hand. We kept up this routine until one cool autumn Saturday. On that day, Shadow rode quietly in his new cat carrier to the vet's for a checkup and vaccinations. Now, it was his turn to adapt to a major life change, because Shadow was moving indoors.

At a time when the traumatic physical changes in my life caused me to think I had little to give, Shadow taught me that I could still nurture. I believe that his adjustment to indoor life was natural and relatively easy because, after all, he was meant to be there.

Shadow found a way to remind me about his role in my life. I mentioned at the beginning of this story that I listened to a national news program in which the clerics talked about angels. I scratched Shadow's head that morning as I turned off the television and asked him, "Do you remember when I used to say, 'Go with God, Shadow'?"

His response to my question astounded me.

Shadow opened his eyes and gazed solemnly at me for a moment. Then he stretched a paw and placed it gently on my heart. And I wondered how I could once not have believed in angels. Especially ones whose wings are hidden beneath fur.

from ANGEL ANIMALS

The Eagle's Answer

BROOKE MARTINI

Our summer escape and means of relaxation had always been the lake that we live on. We actually used the lake for all seasons; swimming in the summer, fishing in the spring and fall, and ice skating in the winter.

On a lazy summer day not too long ago, my mom and I had been discussing facts and feelings about the divorce she and my dad were going through. Living in the situation was exhausting. I would simply try to forget that it even existed, since I was over 21 and trying to begin a life of my own. The conversation on this day was exasperating. We were asking questions that neither one of us could answer. Questions such as, "How long can this go on?" "Am I doing the right thing?" "Why does it have to be this way?"

I didn't want to discuss the matter any further and we both fell silent. Only a few minutes later, as we were floating in the water on a couple of air mattresses, we saw a big, beautiful eagle soar over our house and circle us on the lake. It only stayed a minute or two before disappearing back over our house. It never flapped its wings, it never made a sound.

My mom and I were awestruck. One of my mom's favorite verses is

Isaiah 40:31: "Those who wait upon the Lord will renew their strength. They will soar on wings like eagles; they will run and not grow weary, they will walk and not be faint" (NIV).

God spoke to us that day through one of His beautiful creations. We immediately knew that while we still had so many questions, we must wait for the answers to come in His time. For when we have persevered, the difficulty we once knew will be gone and we will have gained strength.

It has been almost a year and the trying family situation we lived in seems to be coming to a close. Some of our questions remain unanswered, but friends around us who don't know our eagle story have told us that when the difficulty is finally over, we will soar. We often think of that eagle and are continually reminded to wait for God's timing, not our own. How awesome is our Creator!

Black Magic

DIANE M. CIARLONI

I was the only one in my family with a "That Ol' Black Magic" passion for horses. Actually, I was the only one in my family with a passion for animals...period. My parents assumed the "Okay, you may have them if you'll care for them, and if we can afford to feed them" attitude. My brother certainly didn't dislike them but, overall, he was one of the "ho-hum" variety. And my sister...well, let's just say we were different.

I had one horse, a beautiful Tennessee Walker named Bob. Then, a few days following my fourteenth birthday, a neighboring friend told me about a black mare.

"She's really pretty," he said, "but she's wild. She's been running on about 40 acres with a dozen or so mules. The guy who owns the land told me she's been there at least three or four years, which is why she's so wild. He also told me her owner hasn't paid rent in 18 months or more."

I knew there was a point to this story, and I also knew he hadn't made it yet. I was familiar with all of Robert's patterns. He was 17, with a flair for the dramatic. I always thought he used it to draw attention away from the birth defect that burdened him with a left arm that was nothing more than an abbreviated, wilted-looking appendage.

I waited.

"Anyway, Mr. Burns—he's the one who owns the place—told me we can have her if we can catch her."

"What do you mean 'have her'?" I queried.

He shook his head. "I mean just what I said. We can have her. Free. For nothing. All we need to do is catch her."

"And just how wild is she?" I asked.

He grinned and then he laughed. "Pretty darned wild. Wanna' go look at her?"

"How are we going to look at her if she's running wild on 40 acres?" I countered. I knew there would be an answer.

"Because every evening around 5:30 Mr. Burns throws out some hay and a little grain in a corner that's nearest his house. The mare and the mules go up to eat."

I got up from my chair. That was all he needed to signal a "yes" on my part.

I knew where the Burns' place was located, no more than three or four miles from my parents' farm. Most of it was overgrown. I'd noticed a few mules inside the barbed wire fencing, but I'd never caught sight of a black mare.

The trip was short and, just as we drove down the rocky drive leading to the old house, Mr. Burns was walking back to the barn with a couple of empty buckets.

I sat in Robert's truck with the window down, looking. Sure enough, just as he said, there was a beautiful black mare standing in the middle of the mules. At least, she would be beautiful with some loving attention and care. As things were, her long mane and tail were matted with burrs. Her forelock was no better, standing straight out from her forehead in a compact burr column, making her look like a ragamuffin unicorn. Her feet were grown out to the point of being inhumane and, even from a distance, I could see that one eye was infected.

"Her eye," I said. "The right one is infected. She probably poked a thistle in it."

"Just how would you propose to catch her?" I continued. "We sure couldn't walk up to her and slip on a halter and lead rope, especially if she stays bunched inside those mules. Do you know how hard those things kick? And they'll run right over you if they can't get in a good kick."

9

He chuckled. "Yeah, I know that, but here's what I was thinking. It might sound a little complicated, so listen."

I frowned at him, resenting the tone that made me sound less than intelligent.

"He's already feeding them in a corner. We come over here the night before and string a second set of wire so it reaches from one side of the corner to the other and makes a triangle."

I rolled my eyes skyward. I already knew where he was headed, but I let him go on and assume the dramatic role of mastermind. It cost me nothing, and it made him feel good.

"The next day they go into the triangle to eat. We ride over and let our horses distract them. Finally, we jump in and each of us grabs a strand of the loose wire, beats it to the opposite corner and attaches it real loose so you can undo it in a hurry."

Robert paused. He seemed out of breath, as if he'd actually gone through the entire procedure he'd just described. "I get inside the enclosure and shoo out the mules, one-by-one, toward you. You undo the wire and let them go through. Then you rehook the wire until the next one comes."

I looked at him in disbelief. "And you really and truly think this will work?" I asked in dismay. "What happens when about six of those mules—and maybe even the mare herself— charge toward me at once? Surely you don't think a couple of pieces of wire will stop those stub-born-headed things. Who's gonna' scrape me up after they flatten me on the ground? I'll be stuck down there for the rest of my life and, since I'm only 14, that will be a darned long time. And how do you intend to keep the mare from going out the same opening? And—"

He interrupted. "Look," he said in an irritated tone. "This is a free horse. Free! She's not a spring chicken but she's still plenty young enough to have a baby or two, and how many times have you said that's what you've always wanted?

"Sure, it'll take a lot of patience and plenty of work, but I guarantee you we'll get her."

All of sudden, a new thought found its way across my brainwaves. Yes, I definitely wanted this mare and, yes, I definitely would like to breed her. But, I thought, I had someone who was enough of a friend to help me do this crazy thing.

I smiled and shook my head in the affirmative. We got out of the truck

10

and greeted Mr. Burns, filling him in on our plan. He was as skeptical as I'd been but, as far as he was concerned, it was our lives and limbs at risk. He did, however, make us promise to tell our parents and, further, make them promise not to sue him should anything happen to us. We agreed.

Suddenly, as soon as we were faced with nothing but green lights, owning the mare became a reality. I pictured her in our barn. I mentally named her Black Magic because, obviously, she was black and, not so obviously, because it would be sheer magic when (not if) we caught her. I was even thinking about a chocolate-colored stallion named Soldier. Mr. Diggs, another neighbor, owned him. He'd be a perfect breeding for Black Magic. The mare was as good as mine and we hadn't made the first move toward trapping her.

I did, of course, tell my parents the entire story. They assumed their "As long as you take care of her, etc. etc." stance, but I knew they were saying and doing it because they thought there wasn't even a remote chance we'd succeed.

The plan was in place and we began executing it the following evening. The wire was twisted around the gnarled, crusty tree branches that served as fence posts. We used smooth wire instead of barbed to protect my hands since I would be the one executing that part of the scheme.

We were time-synced with Mr. Burns for the next afternoon. We went home. I went to bed and, naturally, I couldn't sleep.

The sun finally came up, the day passed and we saddled our horses for the ride to Mr. Burns. He was just dumping the feed when we dismounted and tied up to the fence. Robert was right. The mules as well as the mare immediately turned their attention to the newcomers. The plan was already succeeding!

We began working, and we worked and we worked and...my hands, even with gloves, looked and felt mangled. We'd both fallen dozens of times, skinning elbows and ripping the knees out of jeans. We were covered with dirt and stickers. Tiny rocks lodged in our shoes. To this day, I have no idea how Robert held up his end of the plan with only one arm.

Darkness fell and we were down to three mules and the mare. Mr. Burns switched on all five of his big, outside floodlights. We sat down on the ground to confer. The main question was, Should we continue or should we hold off until tomorrow?

"If we leave," said Robert, "the other mules will come back and aggravate the mare and the mules who're still in the pen. I'm afraid the mare will hurt herself trying to get out."

"Fine," I rebutted. "If we get the other three mules out tonight, what will we do with the mare? We sure can't load her up in a trailer and take her home since she's about as wild as a March hare. She needs to stay here and be tamed down some. But if we leave her, the same thing will happen that you've already described."

Robert didn't say anything.

I charged into the silence, sarcastically. "Seems to me this part of the plan isn't quite jelled."

"Maybe not," he answered, "but I know there's a solution."

Maybe, but what was it?

It was Mr. Burns who solved the knotty problem. He was pointing behind him as he walked over to us. "That corral over there is old, but it's sound and sturdy," he said. "It would put quite a bit of distance between the mare and the mules, and I don't think she could break out of it or hurt herself."

"But how do we get her over there?" I asked.

"Doing the same thing you've already done," he responded. "String about three strands of wire from either side of the corner to the corral gate. That'll make a sort of alley. Then herd her over there. You'll need to be careful, but you've already done what I thought you'd never do! Besides, the worst that can happen is that she breaks out and gets loose around here. And, even if she did, she'd just go back to the mules."

It sounded good. We picked up the role of wire and cutters but, just as we headed for our target area, Mr. Burns held up his hand. He obviously had another brainstorm.

"Wait," he commanded. "I have some hogwire in the barn. If you use that, it'll seem more like a solid wall." Gee, he was really getting into this. Again, we agreed.

Thirty minutes later the "walls" were up, but we needed more than two hours to get rid of the remaining mules. As soon as they were gone, we ran to the two posts attached to the hogwire. We clipped the barbed wire and kicked it out of the way. The mare, who was covered in lather and wild-eyed, whirled around and looked at the gaping opening. She was confused. We kept our voices calm and started shooing her toward the alleyway leading to the corral.

It was a frightening, rather torturous process for the first 15 or 20 minutes. Then, like a bolt of lightning, she decided to break for the corral gate. As soon as she was in, Mr. Burns jumped into the gap with both arms stretched out to hold her in. In the meantime, we cut the wire and slammed the wooden gate shut.

No one could believe it. Black Magic was actually in the corral. Before total exhaustion claimed us, we hauled buckets of water and feed. Then we mounted our horses and rode back in the dark.

The following day began weeks and weeks of hard work. We did everything possible to gentle the mare. Soothing voices. Special treats. Hours of sitting calmly and silently outside her corral gate. More hours standing motionless inside the gate.

Nothing worked. She refused the treats. She bolted as soon as we took one small step in her direction. She'd been in the corral three weeks and, still, all we could see of her eyes were the whites. And she was losing weight at a nearly alarming rate. She munched only sparingly at the hay, and not even that if she could see anyone around.

"How could she get this wild in less than two years?" I asked Mr. Burns.

"Don't know," he answered. "I guess God created some animals to be wild, and others He created to be part of a person's life. The wild ones have a different spirit. I've seen folks try to force the first ones into the second group, and I can tell you the result is pitiful. You could call it broken. I hate to tell you this, but I think this mare belongs to the first group."

Somewhere, deep inside my soul, I think I heard the truth in Mr. Burns' voice, but I wasn't ready to give up. She had a name. She was no longer just the black mare. She was Black Magic. And she had a breeding to Soldier coming up and, in my heart's eye, I could already see her long-legged baby running like the wind across the pasture. I just needed to work harder.

And I did work harder, and Black Magic refused to respond. There were moments—very fleeting moments—when I caught a different look in her eyes. It was the faintest of all possible hints that she would like to be a part of my life but, unlike me, she'd accepted that it wasn't meant to be. Now that I'm much, much older, I look back and smile. I think of Black Magic and me like ill-fated, star-crossed lovers. The attraction was there, but it would be fatal. It was just a matter of who recognized it first. In this case, it was Black Magic.

I knew what had to be done. Black Magic's coat was dull. Her eyes were sadly lackluster. She was a different horse than the one we'd worked so hard to capture two months earlier. It was time to turn her loose and, somewhere inside my fourteen-year-old soul, I knew it was more than turning loose just one black horse. I knew it was also turning loose dreams and hopes. And, while I didn't realize it then, it was also finding out that, sometimes, the best way to show love is to turn something or someone loose. And I also learned that, sometimes, it's better not to capture something in the first place.

The hogwire alleyway was still in place. I opened the corral gate and waited until Black Magic turned her head toward the opening. She eyed it. She stood still and then looked at me. She watched me and waited. All I did was nod my head. I still don't know how, but she knew what I was telling her. She didn't run. She just trotted down the alleyway and into the pasture where the mules had waited for her for the entire two months. She stopped once and looked back at me.

A kid can't possibly know what he or she is learning as life's equations fall into some sort of sequential order. And certainly no one ever knows what form the teachers will assume. In this case, it was a black mare with burrs in her mane and tail and outgrown feet. I learned about freedom and sacrifice. I learned about caring enough to let go, a lesson I carried with me each time I was faced with putting a beloved animal to sleep. I learned that sometimes people and animals enter our lives for only a short time, passing through the portals of our hearts just long enough to leave us with the results of an important lesson or the seeds of a life-changing idea.

Black Magic was a teacher. I never went to see her again. For whatever reason, it seemed that merely "visiting" her would break apart something very special. It was like a piece of that hogwire keeping us attached to one another and, even though I'd learned about freedom, I didn't want to cut us apart forever.

I never did get a mare and I never did get a baby. But that was just as well since there was no room for them in the corner of my heart that was still occupied by the black mare and her chocolate-colored foal. Now, all these many, many years later, I can still feel the spell woven by that ol' Black Magic.

The Peacekeeper

GLORIA CASSITY STARGEL

he day our younger son Rick left home for the Marine Corps was a heart-wrenching one for me. Beside the fact that I just hate goodbyes, this was my "baby" going off to become a fighting man. I couldn't help worrying that military training would destroy Rick's loving, compassionate spirit. Dear Lord, make him tough, if necessary. But, please, Lord, I prayed, keep him tender. Now who but a mother would make a request like that?

Rick endured the rigors of basic training and Officer Candidate School. Then, after advanced instruction, he was assigned to the Marine Corps Air Station in Cherry Point, NC. There—seeking a little off-duty peace and quiet of his own—he rented a small house out in the country. Always athletic, he looked forward to the solitude of his daily six-mile run along picturesque fields and meadows.

A problem developed, though. It seems that on each farm there were several large dogs. They didn't take too kindly to this strange intruder racing through their territories. Every day, by the time Rick made it back to his house, he was tripping over a whole pack of yelping dogs, most of them snarling at his heels. It was not the tranquil

15

time he had envisioned. Hoping to discourage the attackers, he tried kicking, swinging a stick, yelling. Nothing worked.

One day, Rick phoned home. "Mother," he began, "you know those dogs that have been making my life miserable? Well, I remembered you taught us that 'kindness always pays.' So I decided to give it a try."

"What did you do?" I asked.

"Yesterday, as I ran," he said, "when my patience had been pushed to the limit, I just stopped in my tracks, whirled around to face them, stooped down on one knee, and talked to them in my best 'pet-talk' voice. And you know what?" Rick's voice was smiling now. "Those dogs started wagging their tails and kissing me on the face, each trying to get closer than the other."

"What happened today when you ran?" I wanted to know.

"You wouldn't believe the difference," Rick said. "It was so peaceful! Passing one farm after the other, the whole crowd fell in and ran as usual. But this time they ran with me—not against me. I must have looked like the Pied Piper by the time we got back to my house." I smiled into the phone, picturing my young, still-sensitive son. For Rick had solved his problem. And God had answered a mother's prayer.

The Bird Woman of Moscow

LINDA HOLLAND

ix years ago I began psychotherapy to manage a flare-up of an anxiety disorder called Post Traumatic Stress Disorder. PTSD is characterized by severe anxiety, flashbacks, nightmares, insomnia, and a variety of other equally undesirable symptoms. It can afflict people who have experienced trauma, as I had—a violent event in childhood that forever changed me. I had struggled with PTSD ever since. This time, however, the episodes were more frequent and lasted longer.

Desperate for relief, I contacted a therapist in my area that a friend recommended. I began seeing him twice a week, with contacts by phone in between. And so began an intense and painful journey.

For four years I focused on three activities: go to work, go to therapy, crawl into bed. At times, my PTSD symptoms overwhelmed me, and I would find myself housebound for days at a time; trembling, fearful, pacing, looking outside for anything suspicious, tip-toeing to the front door to squint through the peephole. I wondered if I would ever know peace.

During this time, I found a certain comfort and continuity in my pet birds. I'm a bird lover from way back. I especially like small finches and canaries. I've had as many as thirteen birds at one time. A pair of zebra finches I named Zeek and Zoe built a nest in their cage and produced six eggs. They took turns sitting on the eggs and after a couple weeks the eggs hatched. Two weeks later, the babies began coming out of the nest one at a time, and soon they were full-grown birds. While my life seemed to come to a grinding halt, I watched life go on as usual in the tiny world of their cages.

I continued working at my job, trying to keep up appearances each day, but it felt like a losing battle. I hung on for as long as I could, but after four years, I could no longer continue the drill. I quit my job, pledging to myself that I would either learn how to live or learn how to die—one or the other.

I had some savings, but getting another job took much longer than I had anticipated. My nest egg ran out before a new job presented itself. Finally, I had to make the tough decision to give up my beautiful apartment. Things didn't look good. I didn't know where I would go or where I would live when a friend and her husband offered me an unused room upstairs in their 160-year-old house in a four-corners called Moscow. They had always planned to lend it out to someone in transition. Who knew it would be me?

So I placed my furniture in storage and moved into the room upstairs with my six finches and two canaries. Within minutes the room filled with the chatter of chirps, tweets, and beeps. My friend laughed and remarked, "You're the Bird Woman of Moscow."

The stately brick house sat among sprawling Michigan farmlands. Local history suggested that it was a stop on the Underground Railroad during the Civil War, and that a freed slave was buried in the backyard under the pines. Six old maples towered over the house, forming a U-shape around the front and sides like sentries standing guard over those who dwelled there.

My favorite spot soon became the terrace over the front columned porch, and I spent time there every day. It felt like sitting in a tree house, among the trees. I would watch as the wild birds played and worked in the sunshine, flying from tree to tree, swooping down to look for worms or seed in the grass below.

I was more broke and broken than I'd ever been in my life. To say I had lost my faith was an understatement. I had been raised to believe in

God, and I suppose that stayed with me, but I no longer believed in a god who cared anything about me. He had, it seemed, abandoned me.

One sultry morning in August I stepped out onto the upstairs terrace to sit among the maples. It was one of those sunny days that seemed to promise something good. But my life didn't seem good. The same question echoed in my mind that had plagued me for months: Is God even aware of me? I just sat there letting the maples hover above me, whispering their secrets of generations who had perhaps pondered the same question before me. Suddenly, something caught my eye, something that dropped from high in the tree to the ground.

At first I thought it might be a leaf anticipating an early autumn, but it fell too quickly for a leaf. I got up and peered over the railing to see what it was. Something moved on the ground. I ran downstairs to check it out. As I stepped out onto the front porch I could see a baby bird perched on a fallen branch. At that moment I heard a distinct voice in my head say, "I even see a sparrow fall."

I watched for a few minutes, resisting the impulse to pick up the tiny creature. I knew that if I touched the bird its mother might reject it. I also knew that the instinct for survival prompts hatchlings to push the runt out of the nest. Again I heard the voice in my head, "I even see a sparrow fall."

I spoke to the bird and whistled as it watched me cautiously. Then I picked up a twig and began to herd the little guy around the yard to see if it could fly. If so, it might fly back into the tree and find its nest. But my feathered friend simply hopped across the grass, making several attempts to push off the ground, its wings flapping frantically, but each time it fell back to the ground. We repeated this dance several minutes before the bird appeared too tired to continue.

It became clear that this foundling could not fly. Its tail feathers had not yet grown in and it would not survive a night on the ground. Coyotes or other animals would find it easy prey. So I captured it and put it in a small cage beside my bed.

For the next three days the words, "I even see a sparrow fall" echoed in my mind. It became my mantra, my promise. I fed the tiny bird water and a special formula through an eyedropper. I wrapped it in a washcloth to simulate a nest and it slept until hungry again, when it would pop out of the washcloth, stretch its neck, point its open beak toward heaven, and squawk loudly and urgently. During the day I carried the washcloth nest in a kangaroo-type pouch created from the hem of my t-shirt. Once, as I sat at the kitchen table over coffee with my friend, the bird suddenly popped out of the pouch and hopped onto the kitchen table. It shook the sleep off, looked at me, and chirped.

On the third day, the bird woke me as usual with its cries for food. Once fed, I put it back in the cage. A few minutes later I checked on the bird and found it had died. Its little body lay lifeless on the bottom of the cage. I buried it in the backyard under the pines near the freed slave.

Leaning on the shovel, I stared down at the grave and thought about what had happened. I realized that the message had been delivered in the most personal way. What better choice than a tiny bird to deliver such a definite answer to my question—a bird that had been hand-picked by its Creator.

The ground beneath me felt like sacred ground—not just the graves, but the whole farm. I had come to this place to learn how to live or to learn how to die. Many of my tears had fallen on this fertile soil, but this land had offered me a safe place to grieve and to renew hope.

I still have much work to do. My problems still challenge me. But now I am a believer. I believe that God is aware of me. And it is that belief that gives me courage to learn how to live.

You can believe what you want about my little bird that fell from the maple tree, but if you ask me, I'll tell you that God dropped in for three days to visit with the Bird Woman of Moscow.

How Jellybean Went to Kansas

DIANE M. CIARLONI

 could feel my heartstrings stretch to near-breaking every time I watched Kansas. He was so timid with people and with other animals. So shy he could hardly raise his eyes to meet someone else's gaze.

Kansas was just a "regular" cat. There was absolutely nothing about him that was physically special. He was short-legged and stocky, riding low to the ground. The shape of his head was on the square side, giving him the appearance of a miniature bobcat. He was gray striped. That's it. Just gray striped. No white. Nothing stood out. He did have one unique characteristic, but few people other than myself were ever privileged to see it since it was his belly. Instead of being gray, it was a very soft fawn color with black spots that even the vet found extremely unusual.

Kansas hung around for more than two months before approaching me but, when he did make up his mind, he seemed determined to do everything at once. I was sitting outside on a bench when he suddenly burst from the bushes and landed in my lap. He plopped down and graced me with a lapful of purr. That was it. I'd coaxed and coaxed, but the timid little thing needed time to work up his courage.

It certainly must have been overwhelming for Kansas when he first came into the house. There were other cats as well as dogs, birds and a large black lop bunny named Jellybean. It was enough to daunt even a self-confident cat, which Kansas definitely was not. I thought he would socialize and become braver with time, but he didn't. The extent of his comfortable world was my lap. Everything else was scary.

It was so easy to watch Kansas and mentally change him into the shiest first-grader on the playground. Remember? Maybe it was even you. Standing with hands behind back, tucked away from the other kids but close enough to hear them laughing and see them running and playing. Everything about them seemed so wonderful. You imagined taking that first step and joining them but, somehow, the step never went beyond a thought. It didn't matter that every fiber of your being wanted to join that group. Your feet were tied to the ground and you just couldn't move. That's the way it was with Kansas.

Many, many times I looked on as the dogs played tug-of-war with a strip of rawhide. Kansas watched, inching backwards into a corner when their play-growling became too loud. I watched him as the other cats pounced on a ball with a bell in it, or courageously "killed" a fur mouse. He seemed to accept the fact that he would never be a part of all their activity. There were times when I asked myself if, perhaps, he would have been better off outside and on his own. I could watch his shy misery only so long before inviting him into my lap. I knew that was probably the worst thing I could do, but I couldn't help myself.

The fact that the other cats strongly discouraged Kansas' participation in their games didn't help the situation. There were times when he made half-hearted attempts to be "one of the guys" but he was inevitably rebuffed with slaps or hisses. When that happened, he backed quickly out of the limelight and looked for me. Oh, how my heart ached for the little gray cat! Then, just when I was standing on the brink of despair, Jellybean decided to take things into her own paws.

Jellybean was, in a word, sweet. There was nothing pushy about the big, velvet-like, black lop; but being sweet did not mean she was retiring. It simply meant she was persistent in a pleasing manner and, further, it meant she was extremely difficult to resist. What developed between Kansas and Jellybean was truly amazing.

One day, while working at my computer, my peripheral vision

22

caught sight of Jellybean hopping to Kansas who, as usual, sat on the sidelines of what appeared to be the cat-and-dog olympics. She reached his side, turned around and sat down next to him. As a matter of fact, she was *very* next to him—as in squashed against his plain, gray fur. Kansas looked down at the rabbit, but offered no resistance to what was plainly an overture of some kind. Neither did he try to run away, which, in itself, was rather odd.

Jellybean sat very quietly for five minutes or less. Then she reached over and delivered a couple of bunny kisses before returning to her house. As I said, it was odd behavior and, somehow, I knew more would follow.

That initial contact between Kansas and Jellybean was followed by several more. Sometimes the gray cat and the black bunny paired up seven or eight times during the course of a day. I was fascinated with what was happening but, when I tried to tell friends, no one believed me. Jellybean was actually leading Kansas one, or maybe two, steps closer each day to the other animals. She stayed by his side and, with her there, he never noticed the possibility of what he perceived as danger. Instead, the solid warmth of Jellybean's presence was forming the cornerstone of his newly developing confidence.

23

Jellybean had her own ball, one of those little plastic things with a tiny bell inside. One of her games was to hook her beaver-like teeth into the ball, and toss it with a flip of her neck. Weakly powered by her scant force, it barely "sailed" more than three or four inches but, on a really good effort, it would roll across the carpet until Jellybean hopped over and stopped its forward motion. Once the rabbit had coaxed Kansas more than half-way across the floor of my office, she began playing ball with him. It didn't take long for Kansas to get the hang of things. Before too many practice sessions passed, he and Jellybean were conducting their games at a fever-pitch intensity. Then, after more than two months of Jellybean's coaxing and training, it happened.

It was mid-afternoon and everyone was awakening from naps. That meant new energy reserves available for play. The dogs started off slowly, grabbing rawhide chew toys and anchoring them between their front paws for easier destruction. The cats were prowling, trying to decide what to do. Jellybean found her ball, lowered her black head and butted it to Kansas. The bell inside its frame jingled a merry tune as it headed toward the gray cat. Then, just before it reached him, Doso, a very large Maine Coon, stepped in front of it. He stopped its progress by placing one big, flat, white paw on top of it. When he knew the ball was secure, he turned his head toward Kansas. I could see the gray cat falter. I could almost feel his shyness returning. "Oh, please, Kans," I thought. "Jellybean has worked so hard, buddy. Don't let her down."

I was almost certain I saw Kansas shift his weight and sit up straighter and taller. He relaxed and, just as he did, Doso swiped his paw across the carpet and sent the ball rolling toward Kansas. Do cats smile? How about rabbits? I certainly think they do. As a matter of fact, I would probably take an oath that I saw smiles playing across the faces of Kansas and Jellybean as the gray tabby leaped on the ball and took off around the room with the Coon in hot pursuit. That was the day Kansas joined, and he stayed joined from there on.

Did Kansas leave Jellybean behind once he fell into step with the guys? No, he did not. They still enjoyed their special times with one another on four or five occasions each week. The Bible tells us, "A faithful friend is a strong defense: and he who has found such a one has found a treasure." That was, indeed, Jellybean. She was Kansas' defense for as long as he needed her. She never wavered. She was a treasure who opened his eyes to the many possibilities of the wonderful world around him.

Jellybean and Kansas are both gone, but they didn't leave without teaching me a valuable lesson. They showed me how friendship focuses, friend-to-friend. They showed me how one friend can serve another without feeling a need to say, "Goodness! Look at what I'm doing for you." They showed me that one of the greatest joys of friendship is quietly helping a friend to move into greater, broader spaces without fear of losing him. Plainly and simply speaking, they offered up a definition of friendship; and, I will always thank them for showing me the true meaning of something I once read, something which said, "It is not what you give your friend, but what you are willing to give him, that determines the quality of friendship."

Gifts
from God

Please accept the present that
was brought to you, for God has been
gracious to me and I have all I need
(Genesis 33:11, NIV).

For Such a Time As This

GLORIA CASSITY STARGEL

She came to us with fear and trembling. She left with our hearts. Her name was Misty Dawn.

But wait, I'm getting ahead of my story.

It was on a blustery winter's night that I answered the doorbell's ring to find young Joey Lancaster and his Mom. Joey was holding a huge bundle of long silver fur. From that bundle shone two great big yellow-green eyes on an adorable, pug-nosed face. And draped under Joey's arm was a long, silver plume-like tail. "That's the prettiest cat I ever saw," I said as I ushered them in from the cold.

This was to be a get-acquainted meeting. Joey had proven allergic to cats and needed to find a home for nine-month-old Misty. Being a cat person myself, I agreed to let her stay the weekend—"on trial." I had no way of knowing that we would need her even more than she needed us. Misty wasn't sure she wanted us either and obviously was not happy among strangers in a new environment. She crouched behind furniture or stalked the perimeters of the house, seeking escape.

The next day was no better. I phoned the veterinarian for advice. "I wouldn't adopt a full-grown cat," he said. "They don't easily transfer their affection." And, truth be told, I really wanted a little kitten.

29

On top of that, both our sons, though away at college, urged me to wait for a kitten.

I phoned Joey. "I'm afraid it's not going to work," I said.

He sounded disappointed. "Would you mind just keeping her a few more days until I can find her a home?" he asked.

"Sure, I can do that."

A week later, our son, Randy, called from school. "Mother, do you still have Misty?"

"Yes."

"Well, I've been thinking," he said, "maybe we ought to keep her."

"I've been thinking the same thing," I responded.

Rick, his brother, whole-heartedly agreed and before long, with lots of tender, loving care, Misty knew she had found a home. She proved to be the most gentle of creatures, with the sweetest personality. Within days, however, it became evident that the time had come for her to be spayed. The afternoon when my husband, Joe, and I picked her up at the veterinarian's office following her surgery, we had just left our physician's office where we learned that Joe himself required immediate surgery. The three of us were about to embark on a journey none of us wanted to take.

Thus began a four-year battle against a virulent strain of cancer—a fierce battle for Joe's life. We were swept along in a raging river, its waters wiping out all solid ground. During those first days and weeks, Misty was the one I turned to for solace. She was there when I cried bitter tears. And when I prayed fervent prayers. All during the year of debilitating treatments, Misty quietly and patiently provided a loving presence. When Joe became depressed and pulled away from close emotional contact, Misty's relaxed purr while she curled up in my lap provided comfort.

The following year, as a result of my praying and Joe's urging, I found myself back in college, a first-quarter sophomore after an absence of 27 years! I recall how difficult that first quarter was. Just trying to read the next day's psychology lesson put me to sleep. It was Misty who kept me company while I studied late into the night.

By the time I received my degree from Brenau, I believed God was healing Joe. And, further, I believed He wanted me to write about our experience. So Misty and I began work on my book, *The Healing, One*

Family's Victorious Struggle With Cancer. It took four years; four years with Misty curled up in the top out-basket on the corner of my desk.

Not all was work, however. Being very photogenic, Misty appeared in some rather interesting publications. *Modern Romance,* for instance! In our living room sits a life-sized white ceramic cat. Misty evidently felt some kinship and often visited with it. I managed to get a photo of them side-by-side in the same exact pose, standing regally with tails wrapped gracefully around front paws. You can hardly tell which is the live cat. The magazine featured that picture of Misty in their Pet column.

Another photo op came one night during a presidential debate. I was relaxing in the green recliner, Misty curled up behind my head. As the hour grew late and the debate grew boring, I stood up to go to bed. By now Misty was in a deep sleep, spread-eagled on top of the head-rest. A picture of her in that caring for nothing position appeared in our local newspaper under the title, "Debate? What Debate?"

Misty took part in our family celebrations, too. Best of all, Joe was set free from cancer. Rick married and we gained a lovely daughter-in-law. Then Tyndale House published our book—and there, on the back cover, is Misty right in the forefront of our family photo. For nineteen precious years, Misty was family. Nineteen years of our daily brushing sessions while we "talked it over." Nineteen years of trials, of triumphs.

But, as time will do, it took its toll. One night, while Misty and I sat on the couch watching television, suddenly she rolled off onto the floor, shaking violently. Her eyes mirrored terror—as did my own. I fell to my knees and tried to calm her little body. "God," I cried out, "please help Misty!" Slowly, the seizure subsided, leaving both of us weak—and frightened.

It proved to be the first of several such episodes. And each time, I cried and prayed. And each time she grew weaker. I think she hung on because she didn't want to leave me, and I guess I was selfish. I just couldn't give her up. Then arthritis took over and robbed her of her dignity. Finally, when I saw that every moment was painful for her— how she could no longer even groom herself when she had always been so fastidious—I knew the time had come. I would have to let her go. Her doctor of all those years offered to come to our house rather than put her through the trauma of going to his office. All that after-noon, I sat and held her. I thought back to everything Misty and our family had been through together, especially facing Joe's illness. *Surely God sent you to us for such a time as this.* I told her how much I loved her, how beautiful she was, and what a fine family member she made. "I'll never forget you, Misty."

When the kind doctor left, Joe brought in the little wooden coffin a friend had made. He had even etched her name on top. We placed Misty there on the pillow I had covered in gold satin, tucked her blanket around her, and put in two of her favorite toys. I could go no further. While Joe conducted the burial in the woods behind our house, I sat down at the kitchen table and, with tears flowing, wrote this tribute:

> Misty Dawn—Silver-tipped Persian
> 1972—1991
> Pet, Companion, Friend.
> She asked for little.
> She gave her all.
> The Stargels

At Peace

MARY M. ALWARD

arly last spring my husband and I decided we needed to get away from it all. We wanted to go somewhere where there were no computers, no telephones and few people. We wanted to share a wilderness experience.

While scouring travel brochures, I came across The Homestead, a cabin resort in Ontario's Haliburton Highlands. It promised boating, fishing, solitude and a variety of spectacular nature experiences, depending on what time of year you visited. Immediately we made a reservation for the first week of June—off-season. Most people wouldn't start holidays until their children were out of school for the summer.

We left early on a Saturday morning and drove east through the congested heart of Toronto. From there, we took Highway 427 to Highway 11. Six hours after leaving southern Ontario, we pulled into the driveway of The Homestead. The place looked deserted.

Our hosts were a wonderful couple in their fifties. Their genuine hospitality gave us the feeling of being right at home. In addition, they had a friendly Alaskan Malamute named Frosty who helped ease the ache of missing our own dog.

We arranged for a boat for the next day, unpacked the car and set-tled into our cozy cabin. Early the next morning, we were on the lake, which was a fantastic experience. The crystal water afforded us a great view of what lay in its depths. Large moss-covered rocks, algae and schools of fish made our spirits soar.

The scenery was breathtaking. Several islands dotted the lake. Pine trees seventy feet tall stretched to the sky. A wide variety of birds nested there.

We watched a hawk soar into the sky from an old rotten tree branch. He glided on the wind currents; then, with wings and feet outstretched, hit the water. In his sharp talons was a nice-sized fish. He flapped his wings, climbed into the sky, fish flapping, and disappeared.

It was a beautiful day. Cool enough for light jackets but just the right temperature. We anchored near the shore of one of the islands, and waited.

On shore, a doe came out of the woods and lifted her nose to sniff the air. Then she huffed a soft whoofing sound. The wind currents sent the sounds our way but since she was upwind, she didn't smell us.

Out from the trees came two spotted fawns, twins. They walked behind their mother to the shore and drank deeply of the cold, clear lake water. After a few minutes, the doe lifted her head and looked directly at us. She gave a loud snort, flagged her tail and stamped her feet. The two fawns wheeled and leaped back into the forest, followed closely by their mother.

We stayed on the lake all that day and when the sun began to go down, a family of raccoons waddled to shore. We watched as the mother and her three babies washed and ate their food.

The next morning we got up at 5 A.M. and, following directions given by our hosts, parked the car on an abandoned stretch of road overgrown with grass. We climbed a hill and found ourselves on a rocky bluff overlooking the lake. We sat quietly. Sure enough, just as our hosts had guaranteed, we heard a splash. Our eyes searched the lake. My husband pointed to a marshy spot close to shore. Two otters were skimming along the water. They dove and played for a few minutes before two kits joined them. The family frolicked in the water, playing what appeared to be a game of tag.

When their game was over, they began to dive into the water, time

after time. When we left them, the largest otter, which I assumed was the father of the family, was lying on his back, cracking open clam shells. It was time for breakfast. Not just for the otters but for us as well.

That afternoon we took a drive to Horseshoe Falls. I stood spellbound as the water cascaded into a large pool of what appeared to be crystal-clear water. Mist rose from the area where the falls pounded into the pool, enshrouding the nearby woods in a soft, white veil.

That evening, we sat on the knoll behind our cabin overlooking the lake. Light fog rolled in. The night became chilly. Suddenly, we heard twigs snapping as something made its way through the underbrush about five hundred yards from our cabin. Thinking it might be a bear, we sat, paralyzed.

What we saw next was one of the most picturesque and beautiful sights I have ever seen. A bull moose lumbered out of the woods, down the hill and into the lake. We watched him swim, holding his majestic rack of antlers high. Soon, to our disappointment, he disappeared into the fog. We saw many other marvelous sights that week, but this was the most profound—the most miraculous.

As I watched that moose, the doe and her fawns, and the other creatures in their natural habitat, I felt as one with nature and in tune with the universe. Even now I often close my eyes and watch that moose swimming the lake. The sight has been forever etched on my memory. Each time I do this, as he disappears into the fog, my soul is at peace.

Barney's Gift

LYNN SEELY

arah looked out her kitchen window and sighed. Last night's snow lay in foot-deep marshmallow drifts. To some it was beautiful; to Sarah snow was a hardship. Now the front steps and cement sidewalk would need attention.

Today was Christmas. Sarah saw it merely as one more bleak and lonely winter day. No Christmas tree peeked out the front window. No light winked a cheery greeting and no gaily wrapped presents were to be found in her home.

Her home had once housed a tumble of children and noise, but today it was silent, a stark reminder of what was no more. She had been a widow for many years, yet not one day passed without her missing him—and her only children, a son and daughter, were grown and lived far away. She was expecting a call from her daughter later that day. It would be nice to hear her voice and she would have a chance to thank her for the thoughtful gift, a much-needed check.

Sarah's son was in the navy. He had been away for months and was unable to call or send a gift. She had no idea when she would hear from him again. Perhaps he would be able to call her today, perhaps not. She had to admit that being so alone was difficult at times. Other than the phone call, there was no reason to expect today would be any different from any other. Yet it would be.

Sarah was not as steady on her feet as she used to be and during the winter she worried about slipping on ice and falling. She tried to be careful and always made sure to sprinkle salt on her front steps when they needed it. Once the salt had melted through to the cement, she would make her way down and take care of the sidewalk. No longer able to manage a snow shovel, she used a sturdy broom to sweep or push the snow off a narrow path to her mailbox. She had done so only three days ago, yet it would have to be done again. For a moment she considered waiting a few days before she undertook the task, especially since no mail would be coming today, but decided against it. If it snowed again tonight, it would be too deep for her to deal with.

Sarah grasped the small can filled with salt and headed for the front door. She winced—arthritis pain made even this simple chore difficult. Occasionally the pain seemed more than she could tolerate, yet this morning it was the ache of loneliness that caused her the most distress.

She opened the front door slightly and tossed salt on the top step. Within seconds she heard the familiar, faint crackle that indicated the salt was beginning to change ice and snow to slush.

Gingerly she eased her way outside. She reached into the can for another handful of salt to toss and in doing so lost her balance. Down she tumbled. She hit hard and the next thing she knew she was lying flat on her back at the bottom of her steps. For a moment she lay stunned by the impact, the breath knocked out of her. After a moment, she attempted to get up but her first effort caused such pain that she cried out loudly and stopped moving. A few more attempts to move left no doubt. She wasn't going anywhere! She was unable to get up or even crawl back into her home. Pain radiated down both her legs each time she tried to move. She began sobbing, more from alarm than pain. In fact, if she lay absolutely still, it wasn't that bad. But each time she attempted to move, the stabbing pain stopped her instantly.

How she wished she had worn her winter coat instead of this nightgown and heavy bathrobe. She had boots on, but bitterly regretted her plan to put a coat on just before she swept her walk. The bathrobe was already allowing the cold to penetrate and she was powerless to get back inside her house.

She wondered if this was how she would die. Was she just going to freeze to death? And on this day, of all days? She had no near neighbors and no one was supposed to come by today. Still, fear compelled her to call out. For a long time she yelled for help. She called until she was weak and her voice was too hoarse to continue. Her front door was still slightly open and she could see safety and warmth waiting, just out of reach.

She began to succumb to the cold. It was enticing her to sleep. She decided to let go, to drift off; she was so very, very tired. That was what she would do—she'd sleep for a while, then wake up and try yelling again for help. She just wanted to rest now. She finally closed her eyes and gave in to the deadly desire to sleep.

Sarah tried to brush the annoying bug away. She just wanted to sleep. Her efforts to stop the annoying bug didn't seem to be working. Gradually she grew more aware and her eyes fluttered open. She found herself staring into big brown eyes. That startled her wide awake, though it took a few moments for her mind to process what she saw. It was no bug that had annoyed her and awakened her from her deadly slumber. It had been the wet tongue of a scruffy-looking dog. When he realized she was awake, his tail started wagging vigorously. Then, with one great sigh, the dog lay down right on top of Sarah. At first, the weight of the dog made her want to shove him off, but soon she felt the warmth of his body bringing life back into her.

She had no idea where he had come from. Perhaps he had heard her calling for help. No matter how he had come to be there, she was glad for it.

Sarah noticed that he was wearing an old collar, and as she talked to the dog she read the name tag: Barney. A shiver ran through her. Her late husband had been named Barney. Strange—it was certainly a very strange coincidence. By the looks of him, the dog had not been taken care of. He was thin and his coat was matted with dirt.

Another hour passed and Barney refused to abandon her. Sarah was well aware that her front door was open and the dog could have simply walked inside to a warm house. Yet he chose to stay with her. She had never known a dog could be so brave. His presence kept her awake and hopeful. She talked to him about her life and how she would love to give him a good home. Barney would whine-bark back to her. It was as if he understood her.

She didn't know how much longer she could last like this. She was so cold, except for her chest where Barney was draped over her. She heard the telephone begin to ring in her house. Oh, if only she could reach it! But, of course, she couldn't. But Barney could! What if...?

"Barney—go get the phone." She spoke quietly to the dog. It was absurd to think he would understand, much less actually follow her instructions, yet she felt her heart pound with expectation.

The dog looked at her, unsure what she meant.

"Barney," she said, as she pointed and looked toward the door, "go get the phone."

The dog turned toward the door and stared. The phone was ringing—Sarah knew he could hear it. He didn't move. She pleaded with him one last time and urgently told him to go get the phone.

He slowly got up, took two steps toward the door and then turned around and looked at her, as if waiting to be sure he was doing the right thing. For the last time Sarah pleaded with Barney to get the phone. She knew it was foolish to believe he understood, yet something told her he did.

At last he trotted into the house and out of sight. She heard the phone ring one more time, then it fell silent.

Oh, no! They had hung up. Barney reappeared and stood at the door, unsure what to do next. She called him back to her and thankfully he came. He could have stayed inside and yet he came back! "What a wonderful puppy you are," she said, and hugged him closer. "Poor thing, you tried, didn't you."

Sarah knew she didn't have much longer to live, not in this cold. The temperature had dropped and she knew she had been here for hours. She longed to sleep, but each time she closed her eyes, Barney would lick her face and whine. He was keeping her alive.

Suddenly Barney sat bolt upright and turned his head toward the road. Then she heard it—the sound of a car! It seemed to be coming closer and she tried to yell, but could not. Then a car door slammed and she heard, then saw, the officer. A few minutes later she was covered by a warm blanket. Things happened fast after that. Within twenty minutes she was inside an ambulance, on her way to the hospital. As she was loaded onto the gurney, she asked the officer to look after the dog; he agreed to keep Barney until she came home. The rest of the night was a blur. By morning her daughter was at her bedside and it was then that Sarah found out how the officer came to be at her home.

Her daughter had called to wish her a Merry Christmas. She let the phone ring a long time and then the phone was answered, but all the daughter heard was a strange breathing sound. She was frantic with worry when nothing was said and imagined that her mother lay in the house, injured and unable to speak. She hung up and immediately phoned the police to check on her mother. It was incredible to learn that the dog had actually knocked the ringing phone off the coffee table! "Mom, I didn't even know you had a dog! It's amazing that he knocked that cordless phone over! You know he saved your life!"

Sarah nodded in agreement and explained that she had told the dog to go inside and get the phone. "Except for that, he never left my side. And, honey, there is something you should know. I never saw him before that day."

The next day Sarah asked her daughter to explain to the officer that Barney was not her dog, but that she dearly wanted him. So if his owner wasn't found, Sarah would gladly give him a home.

One week later Sarah returned home, grateful that the disc in her spine, the reason for all the pain, had healed nicely. She was told to be careful when she lifted things. That first day back home she had only one thing on her mind. She wanted to see Barney again.

In the afternoon the police officer brought Barney back. The dog bounded up to her, dancing and wagging his tail. "The owners never claimed him, Sarah," the officer said, "so he belongs to you. He was quite a Christmas gift, I'd say!"

Sarah thanked the officer before he left. It had been good of him to care for Barney. And it certainly showed. Barney had been fed well and washed. His long coat that had been matted and dirty was now shiny and soft. Sarah realized that she loved Barney. He had proven

41

himself to be the bravest, most unselfish creature she had ever known. It still astounded her that he had not left her and gone inside a warm house.

And his name—she couldn't help but wonder at his name. Her husband, Barney, had loved dogs all his life, but after he died, Sarah had not wanted to take on that responsibility. That is, until the day she fell.

She would never be lonely again. The day she came home, Barney also found a home. Some of the mysteries about him would never be solved, but that didn't matter. After all, you don't ask questions about a gift. You just thank God for it.

The Renegade Parrots

LONNIE HULL DUPONT

In San Francisco, a flock of wild green parrots lives near the bay. Nobody knows for certain how they got there—after all, parrots are not native to northern California. One rumor is that a pet shop burned down and these parrots managed to save themselves and become a renegade flock. Whatever the reason, this flock has been living on Russian Hill and Telegraph Hill for many years, flying between the two hills, chattering for those lucky enough to see or hear them.

I lived on Telegraph Hill for many years in the North Beach neighborhood of the city. During my first six years, I heard about the parrots, but I never saw them. I'd heard of people seeing them, but I never talked to anyone who actually had. In fact, I had one friend who was convinced that the existence of the wild parrots in San Francisco was an urban myth.

In my fifth year in San Francisco, I married. My husband and I stayed in my original apartment on the side of Telegraph Hill for the next few years. This was a golden time. We were true, dewy-eyed San Franciscans, in love with our quirky neighborhood, with the billowing fog that burned off by noon, and with each other. We were in good health and crazy about life. We felt unbelievably blessed.

Each morning for exercise, I took walks up Telegraph Hill, one of the city's several steep hills where sometimes the very sidewalks are flights of stairs. At the top of Telegraph Hill, I'd watch the sun rise out of the Bay, illuminating the dozens of Chinese neighbors scattered around the hilltop doing group calisthenics or tai chi. I'd circle Coit Tower, then head back down the hill through a grove of bottle brush trees and bushes of holly. At a short group of stairs, I would always stop, look around at the beauty, and sigh with pure San Francisco pleasure. Then I'd descend the stairs and wind my way home.

One morning, I'd walked my walk, climbed the hill, nodded to some of the Chinese exercisers, and headed down through the grove to the stairs. As usual, I stopped at the top of the steps, looked out over the Bay, and took a deep breath.

This morning, however, I prayed inside, saying how grateful I was for my life. I had had difficult years as a young adult, years full of stress and loneliness, punctuated with the untimely deaths of several people I loved. I felt God had been with me through all of that, and now I felt happier and healthier than I ever had. I felt as if, for now, I was coasting. I stood for a long time, letting the blessings of my life scroll through my mind. Then I looked up at the sky and said out loud, "Thank you, God."

When I started to take a step down the stairs, I suddenly heard such a racket overhead that I stopped short and looked up. There, surging up over the crest of the hill behind me, were the parrots! I was stunned!

I watched the neon streaks of green against a dazzling blue sky and heard the screaming, squawking chatter of fifteen to twenty parrots in formation racing over me, heading west toward Russian Hill. I looked around quickly to see if anyone was around—I so wanted to share this moment! But there was nobody else. Later, my friend who didn't believe the parrots existed, would quiz me in great detail as to what I saw. And she never did believe me!

But I saw them. I heard them. It took only seconds, and they flew directly over me immediately after I had thanked God out loud.

44

And, as that renegade flock of parrots became smaller in the sky, quieter, I heard the Voice inside that I've learned to trust over the years say loud and clear: You're welcome.

One Last Time

TERRI CASTILLO-CHAPIN

 homas Chapin was a hard-playing, spirited saxo-phonist-flautist who performed jazz on big out-door stages and in concert halls and tiny clubs all over the world. He was an original who often said, "Music is my first love." The critics called him "raucous" because he played with such intense physical energy and prowess, sometimes "using yells, roars and howls to charge his performances." Yet when it came to animals, no one could be softer or gentler than he; furry and feathered creatures especially delighted him. They were, shall we say, his second love. So it is not surprising that, in 1997, when he suddenly fell ill at the age of thirty-nine, an animal—a black-and-white stray kitten named Moi—became a comfort and strength to him in his final days.

As a child in Manchester, Connecticut, Thomas had grown up around cats: Boots, an all-black cat with white paws; Felicia, a regal angora with a huge plume tail; and Thomas's favorite, Charlie, a plump, grey-and-white tiger (named after the legendary saxophonist Charlie Parker). Charlie slept at the foot of Thomas's bed during his teen years. I remember, when I first met Charlie at the home of Thomas's parents, how he had a strong and intelligent presence, an

46

independent air. By that time, Thomas was living in New York City, pursuing a career in jazz, and we were dating. I was struck by how dear this cuddly creature was to him. Often we would arrive at his parents' house and the first thing Thomas would do was rush inside, drop his bags and call out, "Charlie! Charlie!" Thomas lit up when Charlie appeared. One year when we visited, his mother spoke softly upon our arrival. "Tom," she said, "Charlie was sick and had to be put away." Thomas's head dropped to his chest and, in silence, he walked to his bedroom and didn't come out until morning.

Shortly after, we were married and lived in a cozy one-bedroom apartment in Queens, New York. By then, Thomas had left a well-known big-band orchestra to form his own group, writing and performing his own compositions. He was happily making a dream come true. "I don't want to play, I must play," he said, explaining that music was his fate rather than a choice. Thomas was deeply spiritual, and he thanked God for the privilege of being able to do what he loved. Through the late eighties and nineties, he became widely known for his work in modern jazz with a trio that included a drummer and a bassist. Through his record label, he was regularly touring the United States, Canada, Europe and Japan, making records and gaining a following.

And animals? They were still a steady component of his life. While our working schedules didn't allow us to have cats, we were able to have two perky, yellow cockatiels, Tweeter and Pai. Thomas taught them words and, by whistling, he would imitate their irrepressible melodies and squawks. As for cats, they still surrounded him: in the streets; darting in and out of alleys; at rehearsal spaces; at friends' homes; and on the road. He'd find them, play with them and adopt them on the run. He even wrote and recorded tunes that captured the spirit of the animals he had known and loved.

Thomas was now busier than ever, at the top of his form. He was cited as "one of the few jazz musicians of his generation to exist in both the worlds of the downtown, experimentalist scene and mainstream jazz." Then on one trip abroad, he unexpectedly fell ill. When he returned home, he was diagnosed with leukemia. This was stunning news, but even that could not keep him down. He brought that raucous playing spirit, along with his faith, to battle the disease. During his many months undergoing chemotherapy, he inspired his own doctors and nurses. He wanted to be back onstage playing, doing what he loved.

After three months of enduring some of the most punishing days a human being could suffer, he was in remission and returned home. It was Good Friday. We both had so much to be thankful for; it was one of our happiest times. While a long road still lay ahead, the doctors said, "Live your life. Play music." In between treatments, Thomas performed again in clubs and at outdoor summer concerts. At home, he read, listened to music and occasionally tried to compose, surrounded by the cockatiels who cheered him and whose sounds and antics inspired in him fresh ideas.

Then at the end of summer, he received discouraging news. The leukemia was back and there was little more the doctors could do. "I want to live. I want to grow old with you. I want to play again," Thomas said to me. We mustered all of our energies and looked into alternative therapies and clinical trials. These were not the easiest of days, yet we had so much: our faith, our families and friends, each other. Thomas maintained a rigorous spirit and optimism. These days he wasn't playing music onstage; the instrument he now played was himself. His generosity, courage and humor were the notes coming out of him, and people—even strangers—were attracted to him. Often doctors and nurses called or stopped by the house to say hello, and former hospital roommates would phone him.

Between the new treatments and outpatient visits, Thomas spent most days in the sunny, back room of our apartment—his music room—that overlooked a neighbor's small garden. We had to ask Thomas's father to come and take the cockatiels away until Thomas was better. His father took the birds to a children's museum near their home in Connecticut where they were welcomed and cared for.

It was late fall and the days were shorter. The house was quiet without the birds. Treatments were continuing. Thomas was frail. One day I found him in the music room, sitting with the saxophone on his lap, tears in his eyes. "I just want to play again," he sighed. And then, as if knowing some truth that hadn't yet registered with me, he said, "I want to play one last time."

As the weeks passed, I began to feel the weight of the illness overtaking all of our long, hard efforts. I could see Thomas's fatigue; this was to be one of his most challenging periods. Yet, he wouldn't give up. The desire to play music again fueled his fight. One day he stood at the window overlooking a neighbor's house. "Come quickly," he called. I ran over and stood next to him, looking out. He pointed to a small black-and-white kitten we'd never seen before frolicking in the garden. The energetic darling was making such a fuss, jumping high to catch a squirrel scampering up a tree trunk, darting between flower bushes and having a...well...raucous time in the garden. Thomas was mesmerized, laughing at the entertainment. The next few mornings it was show time for the cat and Thomas was the audience. Afterward, Thomas would return to his piano and play with renewed concentration.

One morning Thomas got dressed and said, "Let's go outside and find the kitten."

"I don't think so," I replied. "You know stray city cats aren't very friendly."

But Thomas was already out the door and I was trailing behind him. When he reached the neighbor's yard, the kitten—from nowhere—came bounding into his arms. Thomas just laughed as the kitten rubbed up against his face. It was as if these strangers were old friends.

Day after day, Thomas would go out to greet the kitten. One day he learned that our building superintendent had adopted the kitten and let her wander in the basement. That became the new rendezvous for Thomas and the kitten, now named Moi by our super's children. "We don't know where she came from," the kids said while feeding her milk.

The leaves started falling off the trees, Christmas and blustering snows came. Thomas was walking more slowly now, but having his friend in the basement somehow made things easier. Moi was becoming a very special presence to both of us and we talked about keeping her ourselves. But life was too erratic now; we first had to get Thomas's health and strength back.

It was February; the snow lay packed under minus temperatures. A year had passed since Thomas had fallen ill. Musicians from his home state planned a benefit concert for him in his parents' hometown. For weeks the event was written about in the local papers and announced over the radio. By now Thomas had grown quite weak. "I want to attend the concert," he told me and the doctors. They weren't sure that being three hours away from them was a good idea. But on the day of the concert, the doctors agreed to let him go. Thomas, who had not been anywhere in months, was overjoyed. A friend came to drive us. Before we left the apartment, Thomas tucked into his bag the silver flute his parents had given him for graduation. He went downstairs to see Moi. She wiggled playfully under his embrace. "Goodbye, Moi," he said, hugging her close. "You be a good girl while I'm gone."

We left the concrete sidewalks and dense surroundings of our city dwelling and breathed in the fresh, cool air and wide, open spaces of the approaching country. Arriving in the Connecticut neighborhood of his childhood, Thomas perked up at the sight of the familiar scenery: snow-covered fields where he cross-country skied as a child, hills and woods full of tall trees, winding trails and icy brooks. He had hiked there often and found treasured solitude among the birds, the squirrels and deer. When we arrived at his parents' house, he didn't go in immediately, but walked on the frozen ground and among the trees in the yard. He stopped and listened to the song of a bird. I think Thomas could have stood there forever.

We were in the kitchen sipping hot tea with his family when Thomas's father asked, "Would you like to see the cockatiels over at the children's museum?"

"Yes!" Thomas cried, and jumped up to get his jacket.

We drove over. It had been more than six months since we had seen the birds. When Thomas put his face to the cage, Tweeter and Pai began squawking and flapping their wings excitedly. They recognized him! He called out their names, gave his signature whistle, and they answered. A little improvised concert was happening. The museum staff gathered around. We all laughed at the sweet scene. Thomas opened the cage and put his finger up to Pai; she jumped on. He brought her to his face and they played "nosey"—something they often had done. Meanwhile, Tweeter happily flew out and circled the room, singing. The reunion was enchanting and joyous. Before we left, Thomas spoke to the birds, giving them his gentlest goodbye.

That night, Thomas dressed in his favorite billowy white cotton shirt, jeans and boots. His parents drove us to the concert hall. The show had begun, and we were brought to the wing of the stage where we watched the various bands perform and saw the audience. His parents and brother sat in the hall near the front. The auditorium was filled, with standing room only. We were touched by all of the wonderful music and heartfelt tributes. Meanwhile, rumors spread through the hall that Thomas might play. No one knew for sure, least of all myself. Then during intermission, Thomas—moved by all of the music and love he felt—said to his band members, "I want to play."

When the second half of the program started, they called Thomas to the microphone. As he slowly walked across the stage, the audience stood and applauded; many had tears in their eyes. Thomas, too. Most had not seen Thomas for more than a year. He thanked everyone for their support and expressed his love. "I probably have breath for only ten minutes of good sound," he half-joked to the audience. Then he raised the flute to his lips; he played for a full twenty minutes. That giant spirit, which he had always been onstage, came to life. With overwhelming power, he played the most exquisite ballad: each note clear and articulated; a melody haunting and soaring. The tune was a favorite he had composed called Aeolus (God of the Wind). When it was over, everyone stood, breathless, clapping and crying. Thomas looked out as if he were memorizing every single face that was in the hall. Then he smiled, put his hands to his heart, and took a bow.

At his parents' house, Thomas, while uplifted by the evening, was exhausted. It was late, but after a warm bath, I put him to bed. He slept comfortably. In the morning, he awoke with a fever, and the next day he was admitted to the hospital. It was pneumonia. We both knew this was the end. "I'm at peace," he told me, "because of Sunday—." He meant the night of the concert when he had played one last time. We said what were to be our last "I love you's." Then Thomas was placed in intensive care and ten days later he passed on. He died doing what he loved and fulfilling his deepest wish to play. Not because I want to play, because I must.

* * *

Nine months after Thomas had died, the building super came to the apartment to fix a bathroom pipe. He spoke of Thomas and how much he had liked him. He had seen Thomas perform once, he said, and had enjoyed it very much. As he was leaving, he paused in the doorway. "By the way, do you remember Moi, the kitten that lived in the basement?" he asked. "Well, right after Thomas died, she just disappeared."

Some days I imagine Thomas, over there, playing some raucous jazz, with Moi turning somersaults at his feet. Thomas is laughing, doing what he loves.

Special Messengers

See that you do not look down on one of these little ones. For I tell you that their angels in heaven always see the face of my Father in heaven (Matthew 18:10, NIV).

Holy Cow

JODY SEAY

he calf was dying, starving to death, so we stole her, that's all. I don't know why the mama cow stopped feeding her and I don't know why the rancher wouldn't take care of her. All I know is that I couldn't have lived with myself if I'd done it differently.

There was no question among the three of us, Rachel, Judy, and me, as to what we would do, just the formality of a call to the rancher and a note left at the neighbor's. Then we laid the calf's tiny, frail body on some straw in the back of the trailer and christened her "Susie" after Susan Hayward in the movie, *I Want to Live*. Calf in tow, we headed back across the pass to Pagosa Springs.

We bought all the electrolyte solution we could find in town plus a few quarts of Gatorade. We squirted as much of it into Susie as she could hold and then a little more until her eyes bugged and she let out a bawl. Then we placed her on some straw in the corral and waited for something to happen—a miracle, a thunderbolt, *something*—or even acceptance of the possibility of nothing happening at all.

It was the summer of 1984. Earlier that year, my mother had begun her downward spiral from chronic emphysema and even though she'd rallied after one long hospital stay in the spring, we both knew on some deeper level that death would be coming to call soon. Watching this sick little calf grazing somewhere in the pastureland between life and death, I was reminded again of our duty to love without clinging and to let go with honor. I though of my mom and a deep sadness settled over me.

The sadness clung tight, so I took off up the mountainside to find a place to pray. Buddy, the Border Collie, followed. "What does he want?" I thought as I climbed and Buddy followed, leaping from ledge to log to rock along with me as I cried out my anguish in the canyon and prayed for help to heal the wound inside of me.

Then, without preamble or warning, I understood that Buddy was my help—a furry little black-and-white acolyte waiting twenty feet away from each altar I chose. He was sent on this day to help me, obeying a voice deeper than the canyon and lighter than the mountain air—a voice my own sadness wouldn't let me hear.

Buddy was pulling angel duty and I understood. Peace settled like a butterfly in my heart. I looked at Buddy and he grinned his best goofy-dog grin, ears pinned back, stump tail wagging. Like old, dear pals, we walked together back down to the ranch.

In the corral where Susie rested, Judy's horses were doing the oddest thing. They had gathered only a few feet away from this sick baby cow to make shade for her. As the sun would move, the horses would move, shoulder to shoulder in a tight, equine sundial, with each horse doing its part—pulling angel duty for the afternoon.

Susie stood twice that day and went down both times, hard. Toward dusk, we thought she might die so we carried her into the barn, laid her on straw, and talked to her about the courage and the space to live or to die. We massaged her and talked to her until long after dark. As we slipped away and back to the house, we decided that if she lived through the night, she would make it. Something else we all knew, though, was that we had to be willing to let her go as much as we wanted her to stay.

Daylight comes early in the Rockies and it did that next morning, sending streams of sunlight through the blinds. I scrambled from bed pulling on clothes like someone late for a bus. In the dusty haze of the barn, sunlight shone on Susie's head, held high with eyes clear as she

stood there on wobbly legs. Her black coat, so dull and dirty-looking only yesterday, now glistened with life. I knelt in the straw and put my forehead against hers. "Oh," I whispered, "you are the most amazing little cow." And from somewhere on the softest side of my heart, in that place where memories are held in velvet chambers, I knew I would never forget this time.

Rachel arrived with a bottle and formula to feed Susie and Judy arrived with steaming cups of coffee and chocolate-chip cookies. We sat there in the dirt and straw and laughed at the silly dogs and the snooty horses and we loved the calf and each other, and loved a life that could give us so perfect a moment: the chance to be cattle rustlers and to pull angel duty all at once. And we were grateful.

from ANIMALS AS TEACHERS AND HEALERS

A New Beginning

SARA JORDAN

She was a pitiful-looking mutt, leaning into her wire cage door at the animal shelter, straining for us to pet her through the mesh. She was silent, in contrast to all the animated barking of the other dogs in the neighboring kennels. She only looked at us imploringly with great big brown eyes. "Save me," she seemed to be saying. Mostly black Lab, partly unknown, she was frizzy and dirty, abandoned because she "pulled too hard" on the leash.

"She'll outgrow that," my husband Dave and I said to each other confidently. We didn't learn until much later that it was not merely a behavior characteristic of a barely year-old dog, but sheer enthusiasm and strength of spirit that made her forever lunge forward on the leash. If one is lucky, these are qualities that should never be outgrown. Bear taught us that.

"Bear? That's a dumb name for a girl dog," we said. But she answered to it, nevertheless, the only remnant from an owner who had kept her less than a year and dumped her off with no more than an obligatory information card. So Bear she was and is. Come to think of it, it suits her well. She's black as coal, other than a dash of white on her chest and one front paw. She's all chops and paws and hind end and love.

"What's the red ribbon on her cage?" Dave asked the shelter attendant. We noticed she was one of a few dogs that had one on the cage door.

"Oh, that means she doesn't have much time left," the attendant answered while mopping the floor.

"What do you mean?" I asked, although I already knew that they could keep each dog only twenty-one days before they euthanised them. Bear's clock was ticking.

The attendant read the information card on Bear's cage. "Actually, this dog was supposed to be put down this morning. We've got somebody new working here, though, and he accidentally put her back in the cage after he cleaned it, so we figured we'd wait until tomorrow."

Tears came to my eyes. Death had come for Bear that day and she hadn't even realized her narrow escape. How could we not take her? Bear had borrowed time and kept the change. This was a dog that could teach us a lesson in the richness of life and its bald-faced fragility. This was a dog that had come face to face with the harsh realities of life and still pulled hard on the leash. She was ours.

The first order of business was a bath. Rivulets of dirt and dust poured from Bear in our bathtub that night. Afraid at first, she began to enjoy the bath and the feeling of being clean and cared for. Who would've known that underneath it all Bear had a thick, shiny coat of fur?

We put a collar on her and officially claimed her as our own. She seemed proud of her new status and really came alive. This dog that had been so quiet at the shelter found her voice quickly and often. We took her to the park where she ran freely back and forth between us. Bear was a new dog, all right.

Six-and-a-half years later, we cannot imagine life without Bear. She sleeps on my feet now as I type, unaware that I am once again remembering her rocky start in life. She is also unaware of how essential her existence is to me in contemplating my own life. God brought us to the animal shelter that day by happenstance, to save a dog that should have died before we even saw her. God also sent His only Son, Jesus Christ, to save a world that was unaware of its precarious position on the edge of death. We are all dead in our sins, but through the salvation of Jesus we are washed clean, set free, and given a new life for eternity. We become the new creations foretold in 2 Corinthians 5:17.

If we only strain against the leash of sin and open that door to Him, death will one day call and find us missing, too. We will be absent from the body and present with the Lord. Thank God for allowing a u-turn of eternal proportions!

A Bird's Message

ANNE CEDERBERG

t was a wonderful morning in the garden. I'd weeded and was ready to leave, but weeding seemed unrewarding. I wanted something fun to bring home. I saw the mustard plants, which had all formed seeds, and wondered if they were ready to harvest.

I walked over to get a closer look. It was too early to harvest the seeds, I thought. The lower pods had not only turned brown but had shed their seeds. They seemed to have been gnawed at, as though an insect or something had been eating them.

Should I pull up the mustard plants? There were so many. What could I do with so much seed, a big enough supply for years to come? While I pondered what to do, a bird flew within an inch of my forearm as if he were going to land on me. The bird fluttered to about a foot in front of me and hovered. In midair, he turned to look at me. I flinched, startled by his closeness. In response, he flinched too and flew to a nearby branch.

After he perched on the tree, the bird immediately looked at me. I greeted him, telling him how beautiful he was and that I felt honored to be treated like a natural landing pad!

The bird flew to another stake nearby. Again, he turned and looked at me, his red-violet breast and plumage glowing like a jewel in the midday sun. Then he soared to a neighbor's garden, where the mustard plants were in an earlier, flowering stage. He landed on one of the delicate plants, yet barely bent it. The bird looked at me and began to hop around on the plant top. He'd try to eat the seeds, then look at me, and try again. He wasn't having much luck because the seeds weren't developed.

Suddenly, I got the message!

The birds need and want seeds from my mustard plants. One of them came as a great messenger to let me know that the garden wasn't only for me and that I'd been looking at it only from a human's perspective. Needless to say, all the mustard plants with their seedpods remained! The bird messenger taught me that I don't know all the mysterious interactions happening in my garden. A little bird helped me to trust that everything has a purpose, whether I understand it or not.

from ANGEL ANIMALS

The Bobcat

LYNN SEELY

T he summer I was seventeen will always be remembered as the summer of the bobcat. I was on my own and looking for a job—any job. I noticed a flyer that advertised "Carnival help wanted. No experience needed."

As I followed the directions printed on the handbill, I reflected on my situation. The way I saw it, being fresh out of high school and almost broke did not leave me many choices. And my old car wasn't going to last much longer, either. I yearned to be a writer, yet I could not see how that would ever happen. College, my stepping-stone to realizing my goal, seemed an impossible fantasy. No—my dream was never going to happen, and the sooner I realized it, the better.

I arrived on the outskirts of town where the carnival was set up and in a few minutes was speaking with Gert, the owner. I asked if she still needed someone. She did. She asked if I could start immediately. I could. She hired me at once. The entire process had taken only a few minutes. She went on to explain what my job would be as we walked around. It had not occurred to me to ask.

I was to sit in a booth for a few hours each night and sell tickets. All

63

my meals were free, I had a trailer to sleep in, and I would be paid a little something each week.

That night the carnival seemed pleasant enough and I was relieved to be settled somewhere. Lively, foot-tapping music played everywhere. Aromas of cotton candy and other delicious things wafted through the air. Bright lights twinkled and created a festive illusion. Children squealed with delight as they twirled and tilted in giant tea cups or rode on the other carnival rides.

People who worked at the carnival were known as "carnies," and they seemed to be friendly, open folk, with one exception—Gert's husband. He seemed surly and I decided I'd stay as far away from him as possible.

The second day I was with the carnival I wandered over to the "Wild Dangerous Animals Exhibit" tent. Many vividly painted posters near the entrance proclaimed that wild creatures were inside. Curious, I decided to investigate. It was a sad sight: examples of once-living creatures were stuffed and on exhibit. They were in various stages of disintegration. Most were moth-eaten and covered in dust. The largest was a black bear that stood in an unnatural pose, waving a supposedly warm welcome to all who entered. Beyond the bear were other stuffed animals, all dilapidated. The tent had live exhibits, too: a variety of snakes, housed in dirty glass aquariums, were displayed on long wooden tables. But it was what I saw at the very back of the tent that riveted my attention.

In an old rusted cage, no bigger than four feet wide, was a live animal. The hand-written scrawl above the cage read "Rare Dwarf Lion," but it was, in fact, a bobcat. Her cage was filthy. She had no water or food and the only bedding in it was moldy straw that she had been forced to use to relieve herself in. The stench was overpowering.

As I looked at the bobcat I felt immediate kinship as well as profound sorrow at her plight. To her, at our first meeting, I was the enemy. She could not flee, although every instinct compelled her to do just that. She shrank back, exposed white fangs and laid both ears flat. Unblinking hatred glared in her eyes.

I knew something about bobcats. My grandmother had rescued a very young bobcat back in 1920. She would reminisce about Bobbie, as she came to call him, and I would happily listen as she told me of his many antics and habits. Bobbie never saw the inside of a cage.

Ultimately, he took his leave when he was ready. He returned to the Everglades—to live free and wild.

I had learned to have a deep respect and love for this much-misunderstood species. Through reading, I learned quite a lot about the bobcats that inhabited Florida, as well as their western cousins. Bobcats—if given the choice—could survive and even flourish if they were in the right habitat. Even those that had been hand-reared.

I began visiting the bobcat after everyone else was asleep. I told no one. From around 2 A.M. until the sun came up, I would visit with her, then I would sleep during the day. I decided to name the bobcat Millie.

On my nightly visits I would bring her food and water. Since I could not open the cage, I would shove bits of meat through the bars and pour the water into her dish with the help of a funnel. At first she shrank back and acted much as she had the first time I saw her. But as time wore on, she began to trust me. I'd talk to her and sometimes sing softly. And one glorious night, she came to the edge of her cage to greet me as soon as I entered the tent. Her little stumpy tail wagged back and forth slowly, a sign she was happy. From that night on, I knew we were friends.

Sometimes she would playfully shove her paw through the bars when I waved a string back and forth. At times it was hard for me to remember that she was a wild creature. She seemed gentle as a house cat during my visits. Perhaps this was partly due to the fact she was still a young bobcat.

One evening after I had been visiting her for a few hours, I heard someone approach the tent. I darted behind a stack of boxes and hid. Gert's husband stumbled in. He was drunk. He headed for Millie's cage and once there, he banged on it loudly. The tone of his voice left no doubt how much he disliked the little bobcat. I had to stifle the impulse to leap out and confront him.

I watched silently as he unlocked the cage and scraped out some of the soiled straw. He then shut the cage and hung the padlock on, then turned and staggered off. He had not given Millie any water or food, nor had he replaced her straw. Happily, he also had not locked the padlock!

I came back over to the cage and stared at the unlocked cage door. The idea to free Millie had been getting stronger each day, and before me was the chance to actually do it! It would mean that I would have to leave the carnival, which was not something I wanted to do. Still, I knew in my heart that it would be the right thing to do. It was time to take a chance—it was time to set Millie free.

I reached up and removed the padlock, then slowly swung the cage door open. Millie was watching me intently. I spoke softly to her, just as I had many times before, but this time I backed up while coaxing her to follow me.

I gently shook and wobbled my miniature flashlight. The pencil-thin fluttering shaft of dim light barely pierced the darkness in the tent, yet it was enough to entice Millie. Her eyes became large as she focused on the light. This was a new game as far as she was concerned. She jumped out of the cage and followed the beam, just like a house cat would chase a string while playing. I lifted the tent door up, slipped through, and Millie followed.

I tried to stay calm as we walked along. My flashlight grew steadily dimmer, but Millie continued to follow it. She trusted me enough to be relaxed. This was going even better than I had hoped.

Suddenly Millie froze, her interest in the flashlight gone. She realized that she was free! She stared into my eyes for a moment, then looked off in the direction of the forest. Moonlight washed over the silent grasslands that separated Millie from the dark trees of freedom. Though I could not see them now, I knew that the mountains that rose behind the forest would be an ideal habitat for Millie.

Millie was free to go where she wanted to be—and she did. She started trotting toward the forest. I was thrilled that she was free, yet tears ran down my face as I watched her go. I would miss her. She disappeared into the darkness without a backward glance.

I couldn't help but stare at the last place I'd seen her. I stood there for the longest time. Then I had to go. I had to leave this place and this carnival.

Just as I started to turn, Millie appeared at the edge of the darkness. For a moment we stared at each other. I think it was her way of saying goodbye. Then she was gone again, for good. I knew I would never be the same, nor would I ever forget the little bobcat. I had never felt so good about anything else I had ever done. It was good to set things right. And it was right for Millie to be free.

When the sun came up that morning, I was miles away from the carnival. My attitude and views on everything were forever changed that day. I was no longer the same person I had been. I had given the gift of freedom to Millie, yet I had benefited as much as she did. She was proof that I could change things, that I could make a difference. It was a lesson I would never forget.

I was close to 30 years old by the time I got around to college. One of my classes was a creative writing class. The first week we were asked to write about something important to us, an epiphany. I was pleased with my grade. The professor had written a large A right next to the title—"Millie."

The Man Who Hated Cats

DIANE M. CIARLONI

 heard my husband's truck come down the driveway and stop behind our house. The truck door slammed. My office door opened. And slammed. I heard his heavy trudge climbing to the top of the stairs. He found me in the kitchen.

"I need some cat food to take to the barn," he said without preamble.

I paused. I didn't want to say something I shouldn't. It was too harsh to say John hated cats, but it was also far too nice to say he liked them. As a matter of fact, there were times when he found it a bit rough merely to tolerate them, but because felines occupied a large space in my heart, he did the best he could with the purring, meowing, rubbing things. You know, rather like the old adage of "Love me, love my cat."

"Cat food?" I queried hesitantly.

"Yeah. Somebody dumped off two kittens. I thought they'd wander on down the road, but they didn't. They stayed."

Almost afraid to ask, I said, "When did they get there?"

He shrugged his shoulders. I could tell he really didn't want me to know how long they'd gone without food.

"Three or four days ago."

I cringed, but I said nothing. I just looked at him.

"I still have mice over there, ya' know. That's why I didn't do anything about them. I thought they might make a couple of good barn cats."

I nodded my head in the affirmative. "I'll get your food," I said. "Do you want me to go with you?" I was dying to see them, but John indicated I wasn't needed.

"Not this evening. I'm tired, and you'll spend half the night over there goo-gooing at them. But, just so you'll know something, I'll tell you one is gray with gray stripes and the other one looks like a Siamese."

"Do you think they're from the same litter?" I asked.

"I suppose so," he said. "They're exactly the same size. I'll bet there's not a quarter-inch difference in their height. And they stick together like glue. 'Course, I don't understand how two kittens from the same litter can look so different."

He was still shaking his head as I handed him a bag of food. I assumed he was returning to the farm to feed the youngsters rather than waiting until morning. I was right.

I had a very strange feeling about this situation. I thought about it while John was gone. He really did not like cats. At our house, it wasn't at all unusual to hear such pronouncements as:

"Diane, Bubba's looking at my boot really funny. Don't you dare let him go to the bathroom in it." Or...

"Diane, there's a cat hair in my salad. Oh, Lord, here's a whole gob of cat hair!" Or...

"Diane, a cat threw up in the middle of the living-room floor."

It seemed almost constant, which is why I wondered about his posturing over this latest kitty dumping. He should have been irate. He should have said things about taking the kittens to the animal shelter which was less than three miles from the farm. But, instead, he decided to feed them. Something was wrong.

Two days passed before either of us mentioned the kittens again. I was the one who broke the silence.

"How are the kittens?" I asked.

"Fine. They're growing but they're still pretty little."

"I imagine they have fleas like crazy," I said.

69

He nodded his head in the affirmative. "Yeah, they do."

How did he know, I wondered. Generally speaking, it's impossible to see fleas when looking from any kind of distance. And, given John's chronic myopia, it would be impossible for him to see a flea unless—unless—he'd picked up the tiny bodies and actually inspected them. Surely not. I honestly didn't know how much longer I could stand being caged in this prison of not knowing.

"You know," I said, "just two or three fleas on a tiny body can really make the animal sick. Maybe I should go to the pet supply and hunt for a repellent that's safe for babies. If you intend to keep them, they'll also need their first round of shots. I'll buy the serum and do it myself. Then, when they're older, we'll need to think about spaying and...."

Oops. I could tell I may have plunged too far into the kittens' future. I was sure John felt backed into a corner. I immediately began wiggling out of the things I'd said.

"I mean, should you decide to give them away they'll be a lot more appealing to someone if they've been spayed and had their shots."

The statement made sense to John's logical, engineering mind. "Yeah, I s'pose so." We both left it at that.

The next day I bought shots and flea repellents but, rather than going home, I turned in the direction of the farm. The suspense was killing me. There was an urgent, physical need to see these kittens.

"John should be gone," I thought. "He won't be in my way. Besides...." My unspoken words trailed off when I spied the tailgate of his truck poking from the leaves of the low tree branches. I pulled quickly to the side of the road, putting the two passenger-side tires nearly in the ditch. I shut off the engine and removed the keys from the ignition in order to silence Mr. Nader's alarm.

"Why is he here?" I asked myself as I crept toward the gate. I'd almost reached the drive when I heard voices. I stopped and cocked an ear in that direction. No, I didn't hear voices. Instead, I heard *a* voice. *One* voice. *John's* voice. Why in the world was he talking to himself?

I inched closer, pushing in to the fence and parting the branches. I felt like an idiot, but I had no choice. I cautiously raised up and peered over the branch that was shielding most of my body. I had to slam the palm of my hand over my mouth to prevent my blurting out a vocal reaction to what I saw.

John was sitting on one of those molded, white plastic chairs. The gray striped kitten was in his lap, on her back. He was scratching her under the chin and saying ridiculous things in a falsetto voice; things such as "Where did you get that dirt under your chin, little kitty? Have you been in the dirt?" The other kitten, the Siamesy one, was draped around the back of his neck. I absolutely could not believe it. I was so shocked that I was basically paralyzed.

I managed to back along the side of the road toward my car. I got in and closed the door just enough to silence the alarm. I wished there was a way for me to get away without starting the engine but there wasn't. I had to take my chances which, of course, I did. He never heard me. How could he? Every nerve and fiber of his being was too engrossed with those kittens to be aware of anything from the outside world.

It was hard to meet his gaze when he came home that evening.

"Did you get the cat stuff?" he questioned.

I said yes.

"I'm gonna' be gone almost all day tomorrow, so why don't you go over there and do whatever you need to do?"

He wasn't fooling me. First, he didn't want to be there because he didn't want those kittens to go running to him in front of me. Second, he didn't want the little buggers to associate anything unpleasant with him.

"Fine," I answered.

It was three or four days after giving them their shots and flea repellent when John came up the steps carrying a squirming gray kitten.

"Something tried to get them," he explained. "This one was running back and forth across the road in front of the farm. It's a wonder she wasn't run over. I don't know where the other one is. I called for at least 45 minutes but she never came."

"How do you know something was after them?" I asked.

"Their food and water were turned over, and this one acts as if she's been badly traumatized. And it's not like the other one not to come when she's called."

I slid my gaze toward him. "You've been calling them a lot?"

Now he started looking downright sheepish. "Well, they had to know when it was time to eat and things like that."

71

"And what did you call them?"

"I called them kitty and then I used their na...."

He stopped, leaving the end of the word hanging. "Name?" I asked. "They have names?"

"What's wrong with that?" he asked with a hint of belligerence. "Why not have names if they're going to be barn cats?"

"That's fine," I said.

"Puss and Boots," he blurted out.

"What?"

"Puss and Boots," he repeated. "That's their names. Boots is the gray one with the white feet. Puss is the Siamese—if we ever see her again."

It took all of 10 minutes for one thing to become abundantly clear. That was, Boots was *definitely* John's cat. He sat down and she tore as fast as she could to leap into his lap. She stood on his chest, put her tiny head about 1 1/2-inches from his face and cut loose with a very loud meow. I couldn't believe how that kitten's display of affection transformed his usually taciturn visage. It was as if a very, very thick veil dropped away to reveal the pores, fine lines and veins of a real face. It was amazing what a difference it makes when a mask is taken off and put away, even for just a few minutes.

I acted as if I saw nothing strange in his relationship with this kitten. "What do you think about Puss?" I asked.

He shook his head. It was hard to know. We'd been without rain for three months, and were now overrun with coyotes and mountain lions. There'd even been reported sightings of panthers. To hear all that, no one would ever believe we lived less than 10 minutes from a major mall; but we were also surrounded by dense woods.

It was two days later when he walked up the stairs carrying a very hungry, very small Siamese kitten. She'd finally come out of hiding, answering his persistent calling.

He was right when he said the kittens stuck together like glue. Puss went running to her rescue if she heard Boots cry and vice versa. They played rough and tumble together. They play-fought with one another. They groomed one another like a couple of baby monkeys. But they were also as different as the proverbial day and night.

Boots was spoiled. Period. She wanted John to spend his time holding her. Not only that, but it was apparent that she felt most deserving of his constant attention. She had a huge meow for such a small body, and she used it constantly to talk to him. Her vocabulary was quite extensive. She had different levels and a different pitch for various "words." Her meows changed from one to the other in terms of number of syllables. And she had a habit of sitting up like a squirrel with perfect balance. It seemed completely natural for her, and she spent a good deal of time in that posture.

And then there was Puss. She was always ever so busy. She had to go here and go there, strutting with great purpose through a room with her tail fixed straight up like a taut mast on a ship. She had practically no meow. It was as if it was scared out of her whenever she was forced to flee from whatever tried to get her. She sounded like a small, fragile bird making tiny chirps. That was it. She exhibited her own brand of affection and attention, but she was nothing like Boots in that department. For one thing, she absolutely did *not* want to be held. Try it and she fought like a mini-tiger. She did, however, like to come up to one of us, press against an ankle and arch her back. We learned she was telling us to scratch her backbone. As we did, she would squirm to her side and then to her back, presenting her vulnerable underside for scratching and gentle patting.

It was difficult to determine who grew the most, John or the kittens. Oh, sure, they became physically larger but, in a way, so did he. He seemed to bloom and blossom, with the mask moving back into place less and less frequently. And, gradually, they began growing emotionally but, again, so did he. He learned that a creature whom he once hated (or at least intensely disliked) was able to bring out good and beautiful feelings. Might there not be other creatures—other people—who would do the same? Creatures and people who may have been intensely disliked?

Does God not, truly, work in mysterious ways? Is it not truly mysterious how such a powerful Being used two tiny, mewing kittens to transform a very large man who hated cats?

The Lady Wore Black

THOMAS PEEVEY

 ou'd better come home at once," my wife said anxiously from the other end of the phone. "Lady collapsed while eating her supper, and can't get up."

"I'll leave right away," I told her. A quick explanation to my boss, and I was leaving for home. Lady had been ailing for several months now, and it was very important that I be with her when her time came.

It's funny how memories flood back. On my drive home, I remembered the first time I saw Lady. I had gotten her seventeen years earlier, shortly after my arrival from England. I was working on a small thoroughbred horse farm near Lexington, Kentucky, and I mentioned to a coworker that I wanted a dog. Carlos gave me a smile and said he knew of a dog for me. A friend of his was leaving for Florida and couldn't take his dog with him.

I met Lady that evening. A dog with a smooth shiny-black coat, pointed ears and muzzle, and a long tail, she weighed about thirty pounds. What was she? I never knew: Maybe a cross between a Corgi and a Labrador? A friend thought she might have a bit of Schipperke. Lady was never a dog that liked a lot of patting, but she was very knowing. I'm convinced that she sensed my loneliness and took it upon herself to be my protector and companion from Day One.

The farm I worked on was very animal-friendly. The next morning, Lady followed me down to the barns from my trailer on top of the hill. She'd lie in the corner of each stall as I cleaned them out. She loved to play tug-of-war with the rope shanks as I went out into the fields to bring the horses in for their feed.

Lady had a gaiety and love of life about her that made her such a good friend. She would have "puppy fits," running around the fields in big circles, chasing birds, barking and making me laugh. I'll never forget the time when she was playing with two puppies that strayed onto the farm. She ran from them, zigzagging and barking, then looked over her shoulder and did a sudden U-turn between the puppies. In their effort to follow they ran into each other. Lady, tongue hanging out, lay down as if to say, "You guys have a lot to learn!"

Lady loved to swim. On hot days she'd find her way to the farm pond where she'd wallow like a hippo, tongue hanging out, as if to say, "Man, this feels good!" Then she would take off and swim in big circles. When she was through, she would climb out, shake and roll in the grass.

She was a crafty rascal, too. The owner of the farm had some Bantam chickens that ran free and would lay their eggs on the tops of the haystacks in the barns, some twenty feet up. Lady found a way to the top, climbed from bale to bale, and brought the eggs down gently in her mouth, one at a time. She would carry an egg out to the black-top road and drop it, breaking it, so she could eat the contents.

Late that year, I was having a farewell dinner for a friend who was returning to Ireland. It was late December. The stars glittered against the black sky and it was bitter cold. My feet crunched on the frost on the wooden deck. I had fired up the charcoal grill that stood on a waist-high stand outside my trailer, and Lady watched me intently as I placed four pork chops over the white-hot coals. I waited a few minutes, then turned the chops.

My toes were freezing, so I popped back in the trailer to warm my feet. Lady preferred being out in the cold, and stayed behind. A few minutes later, I came back to check on the chops. To my dismay, I found only three chops. Lady was lying next to the grill, contentedly licking her lips. I couldn't be cross, I was so impressed by her incredible dexterity, balance and tenacity. She had retrieved that chop from a white-hot grill that was higher than she was tall. There wasn't even anything close that she could have stood on.

When Lady was about six years old, I got a second dog, a Jack Russell Terrier I called Betsy. Betsy and Lady got to be great friends. Betsy was typical of a Jack Russell, full of tenacity and joy. Their personalities complemented each other well.

Soon after, I got a good job on one of the major thoroughbred farms in Kentucky. Life on the new farm was good, too. I spent much time driving around the farm in my truck. When the dogs rode in the cab, Lady would sit in the passenger seat, while Betsy lay on the seat back, across my shoulders. However, they much preferred riding in the back where they could bark at passing trucks. Lady particularly liked to bite at the trees as we passed. One day, as I drove around the farm, they both jumped out of the moving truck to chase a skunk in the field. Lady, being wiser, avoided being sprayed, but Betsy got well doused.

Then disaster struck. Like many farm workers, I lived in a house on the farm. One morning, as I was leaving for work, I let the dogs out the front door as I did every morning. Betsy must have seen a squirrel or something, because instead of getting in the truck as she always did, she darted across the road and was struck by a farm truck. The driver, one of my best grooms, got out and picked Betsy up. He was visibly distraught as he carried her over to me.

Betsy was still alive, but she was in a bad way, bleeding from the mouth and breathing very heavily. I ushered Lady back into my house. Then the groom and I left to take Betsy to the veterinarian. Unfortunately, Betsy died. I left her at the vet's office, not knowing quite what to do with the body.

When I got back to the farm, I decided that I would go for a long walk to grieve. I took Lady with me. As she got in the cab of the truck, she looked through the back window and then turned at me as if to say, "Where's Betsy?" I hadn't experienced much grief at that time in my life; and I don't think I was aware of Lady's concern.

I drove to Masterson Station Park, an historic plantation outside of Lexington that has been preserved as open fields. Lady loved going there. She usually ran around barking and chasing birds. This time she stayed close to me, leading me to the back of the park. We walked for miles. I had my head down and was feeling sad when I heard a voice say, "What's the matter?" I looked up and saw a well-dressed elderly man in a tweed coat, tie and cap. He had a trimmed grey beard and a kind face. He reminded me of an old friend back home in Newmarket, England.

Lady sat next to me as I told the man about Betsy. He came over and gave me a gentle hug and said that Betsy wouldn't want me to be sad. I knew he was right. As he walked away, I wondered if God had sent him to me to help me deal with the grief. My family was far away in England and farm life was quite lonely. I wondered if Lady had led me to this spot to meet this elderly gentleman who looked so much like home. After all, what was a man like that doing so far out away from the road?

Lady normally followed me into the house after work. For several weeks after Betsy died she would stay on the porch as if waiting for Betsy. She eventually gave up, but I'm sure she was always perplexed about Betsy suddenly going missing.

I wanted to get another dog for Lady, and a few months later I got a Beagle that I named Millie. Lady and Millie became great friends. Millie was full of mischief. Raising her, and keeping her out of trouble, eased Lady's grief as well as mine.

Shortly after getting Millie, I lost my job. I was allowed to continue living in my house for two months after being terminated. In that time, I spent quite a bit of time off the farm looking for a new job. I would leave Lady and Millie with Thirza, one of my recently hired grooms. Thirza loved my dogs and took great care of them. She took them to lunch every day and bought them a burger to share. Lady would follow Thirza from stall to stall, as she had with me. At three o'clock each day, she would say goodbye to Thirza and walk up to my house to sit on the porch and wait for me. It was as if she were saying, "You are very nice, but I want to be with my dad."

When Lady was thirteen, I bought my own home and began working at a feed research facility. The dogs continued to go to work with me, and my new boss, Karen, became quite fond of them as well. While I was working there, Lady became very ill. She was weak and wouldn't eat. It took several visits to the vet to diagnose hemolytic anemia, a deadly autoimmune disease in which the body attacks its own red blood cells. It is almost always fatal. When Lady was diagnosed, her red cell count was nine. A count of eight is seen only in a dead dog.

She spent five terrible days and nights in intensive care, but I wasn't ready to say goodbye to my old friend. She barely clung to life, but with transfusions, steroids and round-the-clock supportive care, her red cell count slowly climbed. I was constantly on the phone to my family in England giving them updates. Karen inquired daily about her condition, as well.

When I was finally able to take Lady home, I asked the receptionist about the bill, telling her I couldn't pay that day. The receptionist smiled and told me that a friend of Lady's had come in to inquire about her and paid one hundred dollars toward the bill, but wouldn't give a name. I later learned the mystery lady was Karen. My father and younger brother, knowing how much I loved Lady, paid the rest. I felt that they were as happy as I was that she had recovered.

Lady was getting to be an old dog. A year later she had a second bout of hemolytic anemia. At about that time I met up with Thirza again, and we started going out. Lady seemed to approve of the match. It was almost as if she was trying to find a replacement for herself. "Dad," she seemed to say, "We both know I am not going to be here much longer. You need someone to follow you around when I'm gone."

When I asked Thirza to marry me and she accepted, Lady seemed overjoyed. She followed us more closely than usual, as if to share in the joy of the moment. Almost blind and deaf, she looked at me through clouded eyes, as if to say, "About time, too! Now you've found someone to love you as much as I do, and I'll be able to go in peace."

All these scenes came crowding back into my memory as I hurried home to be with Lady. On my arrival, I found my wife lying on the floor next to Lady, comforting her. Lady hardly recognized me. I sat next to her on the floor and gently stroked her. She was nearly eighteen years old, and we all knew it was her time.

I rang our vet, knowing he was unable to come to his clinic due to a recent surgery. He sent his partner, Dr. Coutts, and she was wonderful. She met us in the clinic parking lot, and we stood there in the dark, under the stars, while she encouraged me to talk about Lady. That brought mostly laughter, but also tears. It was time.

We entered the clinic, and I gently laid Lady on the table. I was holding her and my wife was holding me as Dr. Coutts inserted the needle. Lady was still, and we were quiet. After a moment, she slipped away.

Dr. Coutts asked if we would like her to dispose of the body. Remembering Lady's reaction to Betsy's disappearance, I said "No." I wanted to take her home so our pets could say goodbye. Dr. Coutts gave us a cardboard casket and helped us place Lady in it.

When we got home, I put the casket in the back room and opened the lid. Millie came first. She minutely sniffed Lady from head to foot. She gave a sigh, went to her basket and was quiet for the rest of the night. Merry, our tortoiseshell cat, did the same. Then our buff-colored cat, Charlie, gently got into the casket and lay with Lady for some time.

The next day, I buried Lady along with her bowl, her collar and her leash. The animals seemed content, and we all had closure. Lady had been such a good friend to us. She helped me to learn about love, loyalty and just plain having fun.

Buckwheat,
the Singing Dog

MARY ALICE BAUMGARDNER

 t was over twenty years ago that a lovable, golden-haired mutt named Buckwheat came into our lives. A photograph had appeared in our local paper, featuring him as "Pet of the Week." We dashed over to the animal shelter and adopted him into our family, right in time for our oldest son Matthew's ninth birthday.

As we sang "Happy Birthday to Matthew," we discovered that Buckwheat had a special talent. He sang. Buckwheat didn't howl, as other dogs might. He sort of came down on the notes, intoning an "oooh" sound. He traveled up and down his range with that "oooh." He had a certain poise, almost spiritual, as he got involved in the song. It seemed as if there was more than just noise coming from him.

While our three sons were in school, Buckwheat would curl up at my feet as I worked at my desk. He listened with benign tolerance to my classical music selections. But he had a passion for Pavarotti! He came to attention at the first strains of "Panis Angelicus." With his front paws crossed, he would tilt his head back—and totally drown out Luciano. I liked "Panis Angelicus" and preferred Pavarotti's rendition to Buckwheat's. But Buckwheat was so soulful, so intense, I would never silence him.

"O Holy Night" was on that same Pavarotti Christmas album. Buckwheat would quietly listen to the English version. Then, as soon as Pavarotti began in French with "Minuit Chretiens," Buckwheat would accompany him. We never understood why this was. Someone tried to explain that perhaps Buckwheat didn't know the words in English!

We had a friend who was quite a skeptic. He was certain we were embellishing Buckwheat's musical ability. The first time Bill met Buckwheat, I went upstairs and turned on "Panis Angelicus." Buckwheat didn't let me down. Up the stairs he trotted, with Bill following. He positioned himself in front of the boombox in my studio, crossed his paws, tilted his head back...and sang with all his might. Bill was astonished. "You should put him on television," he advised us. "He's incredible!"

Buckwheat's musical interest wasn't limited to vocal pieces. Matthew loved playing the piano, but detested piano lessons. How grateful he was when Buckwheat would join in during those sessions. The piano teacher, who came to our home, was not impressed with a canine accompanist, however, so I had to bribe Buckwheat into the kitchen with dog biscuits.

As the boys got older, Buckwheat broadened his repertoire to include their guitar arrangements. He was quite selective in what he would perform, but he always had an appreciative audience. Everyone thought he should be on television. Were we doing him a disservice by not sharing his gift with mankind?

Buckwheat's big chance came during a summer when the local news was as dried up as the fields. I had been interviewed for the newspaper because I was co-producing a talent show for teens. Although he wasn't scheduled to perform, Buckwheat sat in on the interview. I happened to mention his unique ability to the reporter. Of course, a reporter wouldn't want to miss a chance to hear a singing dog. So, in my off-key voice, I lured Buckwheat on with his old standard, "Happy Birthday." He followed along quite well, drowning out my part of the duet.

Buckwheat impressed the reporter so much that he wrote a two-column article that appeared on the front page. Accompanying it was a large photograph of Buckwheat with my son, Michael. Folks loved it. They were grateful to read about something besides the oppressive heat, and it was a very well-written article.

Several days later a representative from a Martinsburg, West Virginia, television station phoned. Could Buckwheat and I appear on their talk show? I thought my sons would do a better job, but the station manager insisted on me.

My personal apprehension about appearing on television was diminished by my great concern as to how Buckwheat would respond. There was no guarantee how he would act under the lights. Suppose he barked or, worse yet, suppose he wouldn't do anything? I should have refused the "offer" but the boys were high-fiving and jumping all over the place at the prospects of having "Wheatie" on TV. I couldn't let everyone down just because of my misgivings. At least I had the presence of mind to insist that they tape a video of "the singing dog" before the "live show"...just in case.

My television interview went well. Buckwheat didn't bark at anyone. But Buckwheat proved himself to be a very temperamental tenor and refused to sing. I was glad we had the video backup. Buckwheat's television career ended in Martinsburg.

However, our local radio station must have been hard up for programming. To this day, I still don't know where my brain was when I agreed to pick up the phone and go on the air with Buckwheat. I had no desire for the community to know how flat I could sing "Happy Birthday." But I sang—solo. Buckwheat refused to perform.

I couldn't understand why Buckwheat was so provincial. Why didn't he want to share his talent with the world? Why was he so uncooperative? My opinion of him flagged. I hadn't expected him to provide income for the family, but I thought he could have been more responsive. I was disappointed.

However, Buckwheat was a wonderful part of our family for fourteen years. One evening, several years after his death, John, the boys' guitar teacher, stopped by. We all gathered around the kitchen table, reminiscing. I mentioned that I never did understand why Buckwheat would sing only for us.

It was John who put things in a different perspective. John, who sought fame and fortune with his music...who worked menial jobs in order to have more time to polish his stage performance...John, who wanted more than anything to be a successful musician...it was John who understood.

John explained that there are many who have talent and who want to reach the top, to be a star, to bask in the adulation of others. But there are very few, like Buckwheat, who have a gift that they enjoy sharing only with the ones they truly love. They don't need the praise of the rest of the world.

I think John was right. Buckwheat didn't need the limelight. He was content to share his talent with his family and friends, down on the farm. And how blessed we were to have had a singing dog!

In Time
of Danger

...I will be with thee:

I will not fail thee, nor forsake thee

(Joshua 1:5. KJV).

The Quality of Mercy

BIANCA ROTHSCHILD

 nimals have always been part of my life. I love them with a passion. But one special "angel animal" will remain in my heart forever.

I am a lady in my mid-seventies who has an amazing story to tell. Born in Poland, I was a teenager when World War II began. My family always had pets. All of us loved them dearly. When the Nazis forced us to leave our home to be put into prison, we entrusted the animals to friends for safekeeping.

By 1945 I was separated from my family and imprisoned in the Ravensbruck, a concentration camp in Germany. Starving, dressed only in a flimsy uniform, I had to work in the bitter cold. Every day prisoners at the camp congregated in the early morning and waited outside to be counted. One day, while I waited in line, exhaustion and cold overwhelmed me and I fainted. Although two of my friends stood in the long row on either side of me, they couldn't help.

When the Nazi soldiers saw me lying on the ground, they took one of their large German shepherd dogs off of his leash, removed the dog's muzzle, and commanded him to attack. As the dog ran toward me, the prisoners looked on in horror, fully expecting the animal to rip me apart.

But something miraculous happened in that moment.

When the huge dog reached me, he stopped in his tracks. Then he smelled me. To everyone's amazement, the dog, instead of attacking me, licked my face until I revived.

Everyone in the line stood frozen with fear. The soldier who had sent the dog to kill me looked incredibly puzzled. After a minute, I staggered to my feet. Shocked that the dog had allowed me to live, the soldier called the vicious-looking animal back to him.

Those many years ago, an animal befriended me in an insane world of human hatred. I am alive today because a dog disobeyed the command to destroy and instead showed compassion. Was it fate? Was he an angel? I will never know. But to this day I have never forgotten the dog's act of mercy. For the rest of my life I have done whatever I could to save all living creatures.

from ANGEL ANIMALS

The Gatekeeper

GAYLE TRENT

ad you seen Duke, it isn't likely you'd have called him an angel. In fact, not even I called him "angel." I called him "my baby."

Duke was a St. Bernard, a gift to me from my parents on my tenth birthday. I arrived home from school that day and was immediately sent to the garage. And there he was, quite an armful already, but I gleefully picked him up and buried my face in his neck.

Early on, I taught Duke to rub noses with me. This kept me from getting drooly dog kisses, and it was our own special way of showing affection. When Duke was relegated to a doghouse in the backyard, I'd slip outside to sing him to sleep at night. We had a special relationship. He was "my dog," I was "his girl."

One summer night after Duke was fully grown, I went out to refill his water bowl. I retrieved the bowl and filled it at an outside spigot.

"There you go, baby," I said, putting the bowl on the ground in front of him. I hugged him around the neck, and he growled. Taken aback and more than a little hurt, I went to stand beside his house.

"You might growl at other people, mister," I said, as he was extremely protective of me and had been known to growl at others, "but you do not growl at me."

My lecture was silenced when Duke came to me, jumped up, and placed a massive paw at either side of my waist. He emitted another low, menacing growl. I was unable to move, and my dog's behavior was beginning to frighten me. He was my best friend, my guardian. Was he going to turn on me now?

I noticed that his face was turned away from me and that he was staring toward the road that ran in front of our house. As I watched in the direction of Duke's gaze, I spotted a man emerge from the shadows and walk down the road. Duke held me against the side of his doghouse until the man was gone. When he was satisfied that there was no longer a threat, he touched his nose to mine and let me go. As he thirstily drank from his water bowl, I hugged him and thanked him for his continued protection.

Weela,
a Community Hero

RUTH GORDON

f you drove up the road leading to the Watkins' ranch near Imperial Beach, California in 1994, you would have been greeted by a remarkable dog named Weela, a 65-pound, female American pit bull terrier. Officially an American Staffordshire terrier, and sometimes known as a Yankee terrier, the pit bull's unfortunate reputation comes from the men who took advantage of the breed's rare courage by training them to be bloody, fighting tools for unscrupulous gamblers. Without such training, an American pit bull terrier is intelligent, easily trained, strongly attached to its owner, and guardian of its owner's property. The American pit bull is often called "the most courageous animal ever born."

Weela was never taught to fight, nor was she harshly disciplined, so her behavior contrasts sharply with the pit bull's stereotypic reputation for viciousness. Weela was brought up surrounded by an affectionate family who taught her basic obedience and good manners. She was allowed to examine her world of animals and humans without undue restraint. She lived as an ordinary loving and beloved family pet, but her life was anything but ordinary. It was as if Weela had her own destiny and reason for being from the start.

One of ten puppies abandoned and left to die in a back alley in Imperial Beach, California, Weela's start in life was precarious. A near tragedy was averted by a chance encounter. Good fortune came to these puppies when Lori Watkins, an animal lover, happened to go to town to do some errands the day after the puppies were abandoned. Lori parked her car and started her errands, walking several blocks, stopping at the drug store, bakery, and dry cleaners. As she walked past an alley she heard some strange sounds. They were not very loud, but they sounded like the whimpering of an animal or animals in distress. After she finished her errands, she walked back to the alley. She entered the alley and walked slowly in the direction of the sound to investigate its source. Lori was astonished to find a litter of ten puppies, apparently abandoned by both the mother and the mother's owner. She later found out that the puppies' mother was a very young American pit bull terrier that had been bred too young. When the owner discovered that the young mother, almost a puppy herself, was inadequate for her job, the owner decided to get rid of the puppies.

Once Lori discovered the source of the strange sounds, she hurriedly carried her purchases back to her car and drove straight to the alley where the puppies were huddled together crying for food and water. She gathered them up in an old car blanket, put them in a carton she had in the back seat, and drove them home to her ranch not far from the city.

When Lori arrived home with her unusual cargo, the whole Watkins family enthusiastically pitched in and planned how to help the newest additions to their family. They fed them, watered them, played with them, kept them warm and gave them the love they so needed—the puppies had a family of human surrogate parents. It was not long before the puppies started to flourish and grow. From the very beginning, one of the pups, a female, took a shine to the Watkins' young son. She would not let him out of her sight. She slept with him and followed him everywhere he went. In truth, this little puppy, whom they named Weela, adopted the young boy by simply claiming him as hers.

As the puppies grew older and stronger, one by one Lori found a good home for each of them—that is, all but one. Needless to say, Weela stayed on to live with the Watkins family. Finding these pup-

pies in such a vulnerable state led to Lori's special interest in the spay/neutering program of the Humane Society.

Weela grew up to be a very happy 65-pound adult dog. She loved to run loose on the ranch, visiting with the horses, cows and chickens. She was unafraid of all but one of the animals. The only animal that baffled Weela was the goat. She was always terrified of the goat. The family seems pretty certain that the goat never charged her. Perhaps she feared the goat because he always put his head down in a menacing way or because he had such a funny voice. No one knows. For whatever reason, Weela was always very careful to stay out of the goat's way. Weela also had her favorite animals. Her most favorite was a potbelly pig who seemed equally happy to see Weela when she came dancing and sniffing around. They sometimes seemed to have serious conversations about life and their lives in particular.

Weela also participated in all the activities of the human members

93

of her family. She loved to swim and when the family went fishing, she was there. When the family went horseback riding up the nearby trails, Weela followed along. And when the family relaxed, she joined them on the couch, typical of most people's pets.

If Weela was such a typical pet, what made her different? In 1993, Weela became the Ken-L-Ration Dog Hero of the Year, the 40th dog so honored since the awards began in 1954. She earned this award because of the extraordinary courage she exhibited during a California flood. Weela did not just perform one act of heroism as so many other winners had, nor was her heroism solely directed toward her owners. Weela went on countless missions to rescue both strangers and animals over a period of three months. During this time she is credited with saving 30 people, 29 dogs, 13 horses, and one cat, all of whom most likely would have died during the large-scale winter flooding in southern California.

In January 1993, heavy rains caused a dam to break miles upstream on the Tijuana River. Normally a narrow, three-foot-wide river, the dam break caused wild raging waters to isolate both people and animals for almost three months. When the dam first broke through, Lori and Dan Watkins and Weela went to a neighbor's ranch to try to rescue their friend's 12 dogs. Together, they worked for six hours battling heavy rains, strong currents, and floating debris before they were able to reach the ranch to rescue the dogs. The Watkins were amazed at Weela's extraordinary ability to recognize quicksand, dangerous drop-offs, and mud bogs. She worked diligently and never let up. Both the tenaciousness and strength of her bull dog ancestors were exhibited throughout the day. Lori Watkins said, "She was constantly willing to put herself in dangerous situations. She always took the lead except to circle back if someone needed help." Weela's instinctive judgments seemed to be accurate without exception. The Watkins attributed a great deal of their success in rescuing the neighbor's dogs to Weela's efforts.

During the next month, 17 dogs and one cat were found to be stranded on an island. On several occasions, Weela swam to the island, each time pulling 30 to 50 pounds of dog food that had been loaded into a backpack harnessed to her back. This took enormous strength as well as courage. Weela continued to provide these animals with food until they were finally evacuated on Valentine's Day.

During the peak of the flood, thirteen horses became stranded on a large manure pile where they had sought refuge from the raging waters. The frightened animals had become completely surrounded by flood waters. A rescue team used Weela to guide them through the rapidly flowing waters until all of the horses were finally brought to safe ground.

One day while Weela was returning from one of her food deliveries to stranded animals, she came upon a group of 30 people who were attempting to cross the flood waters. Weela became very excited. She refused to let them cross where they were trying to do so. She barked continuously and kept running back and forth, literally herding them to another place where it was safe to do so. Unwittingly, these people had been trying to cross the river at a point where the waters ran particularly fast and where the water was deepest. Weela knew that this was a dangerous spot, so she led them upstream to shallower water where the group was finally able to cross to the other side safely.

After several months, the Tijuana River finally became narrow and calm again. Once the emergency was over, there was no longer a need for a rescue dog, so Weela went back home to the ranch full-time to enjoy life as before. However, her community heroism was recognized. As the Ken-L-Ration's 40th award winner in their annual search for the most heroic dog in the nation, Weela received a certificate of merit, a silver-plated, engraved bowl, and a year's supply of Kibbles'n Bits dog food. Surely, the people she diverted from disaster and the animals she fed when the waters were raging around them will not forget her. Weela's life seemed to have found its purpose and destiny. However, if you saw her today running around the ranch, you would think she was just a delightful but ordinary pet.

from IT TAKES A DOG TO RAISE A VILLAGE

The Lord Works
in Mysterious Ways

RENIE SZILAK BURGHARDT

 am an avid hunter. Especially in the spring of the year when the air is fresh, the breezes gentle, and new "game" is plentiful. More often than not, I hunt in my woods and fields, armed with my trusty *Wildflowers and Plants of North America* book, a camera, and a dog and cat companion. And, yes, I'm a wildflower hunter.

The Mark Twain National Forest covers 1.5 million acres in southern Missouri. Noted for its scenic qualities, the Forest contains much for the outdoor lover. If you hanker for clear, cool, spring-fed streams to dip your toes into, you will find them here. If changing landforms are your thing, you will find peaks, hills and knobs of varying heights throughout the forest. Exposed rock and open glades also add interest to the scenic settings.

Each spring, enchanting wildflowers, ferns, and prairie grasses appear, to the special delight of wildflower enthusiasts. Some of these wildflowers are rare, and even endangered—like the yellow lady's slipper plant, a member of the wild orchid family.

Two years ago, my friend and fellow wildflower enthusiast, Hazel, called to tell me she had heard where there were some yellow lady's slippers growing in the Mark Twain National Forest. "It's in the J Highway area of the forest," she said. "Want to go see if we can find them?"

"Do I ever!" I said. "How about tomorrow morning?"

It was a beautiful, mild, late April morning as Hazel and I drove up to J Highway to set out for the hunt for the yellow lady's slipper. Most of the land in that area is owned by the Forest Service, except for a few smatterings of privately owned farms, which, it turned out, was a lucky thing for two careless hunters!

We parked the car on a side road, and walked into the leafy sanctuary of tall oaks and hickorys. A myriad of plants and wildflowers carpeted the floor, and we soon became so engrossed in trying to identify each one that we lost all sense of time and direction. But what was even worse, we failed to take notice of the ominous changes taking place above our heads—until we heard a noise that compelled us to look up.

"Oh, my gosh, it's thundering in the distance. There's a storm coming," I said to Hazel. "We'd better head back to the car."

"You ain't a-kidding," Hazel said. "And we'd better hurry, too. From the looks of those dark clouds, it will be a doozie!" We turned quickly and began sprinting through the woods in the direction of our vehicle. Unfortunately, our vehicle was nowhere to be found. We had gotten ourselves lost!

After sprinting some more, while the sky grew even darker and the thunder closer, panic began to set in. So we stopped for a minute to rest.

"I can't believe we got lost. I've been in these woods many times and thought I knew the way," Hazel said.

"Sh-h! Listen! I hear something," I interrupted.

"Cock-a-doodle-do! Cock-a-doodle-do" the something went.

"It's a rooster crowing! And it doesn't sound too far away. We must be near a farm," Hazel said. "Come on, let's follow the noise." A few minutes later we came out in a clearing and saw the rustic farmhouse, just ahead. We landed on the farm's front porch just as the first crack of lightning came down, almost at our heels!

A woman opened the door to see who the strangers on her porch were.

"Hi," Hazel said. "We were wildflower hunting in the National Forest and we got lost, and when we finally found our way out, well here we are at your place," Hazel told her.

"Oh, you poor things," the woman said. "You were lucky to find your way out before the storm hit. Come in and have a cup of coffee with me. And later, I'll drive you back and help you find your vehicle."

"Well, it was more than luck that brought us to safety," I mused over coffee. "We heard your rooster crowing and followed the noise. We're sure glad you have a rooster."

The woman looked at us with a strange expression. "Well, if that don't beat all," she said.

"Beg your pardon?" Hazel and I looked at her curiously.

"You see, ladies, that's a young rooster. This morning was the first time he crowed," she said. Then she smiled and added, "Well, they do say that the Lord works in mysterious ways. This just proves it."

He does indeed!

Kimberly's Best Friend

BRAD STEIGER

reg Harding deliberated for days before he decided to buy a cat for his seven-year-old daughter. In March 1991 he had just reached the point where he could afford to move his family to a quiet suburb of Seattle, and he thought it would be nice if Kimberly had a pet.

But Harding had lost several cats when he was a boy. He would just begin to grow attached to them when they would either wander off and never return or would meet with fatal accidents on the street in front of their home in El Cajon, California. He had come to consider cats unstable, unreliable, perfidious creatures—that were also very accident prone.

When he brought home Elvira, a young black female, he had a little talk prepared to protect Kimberly's feelings. He told her that cats were more like visitors than permanent members of the family. Cats should be treated with love and respect, but one should never expect them to stay for very long. Kimberly should not be hurt or take it personally if Elvira just up and disappeared one day.

As the months went by and Elvira turned out to be a regular homebody and a wonderful friend to Kimberly, Harding began to wonder whether the jinx he had always experienced with cats had at last been broken.

"Elvira has brought Kimberly so much happiness," Karen Harding, Greg's wife, said to him one evening. "I'm so happy you were able to rise above your own childhood disappointment in cats."

On the night when Elvira failed to return home, Harding felt he might be guilty of some terrible self-fulfilling prophecy. He stood quietly at the door of Kimberly's bedroom as she asked in her evening prayers for Elvira please to come home to her.

Harding knew well the pain that his daughter felt, and a small voice in the back of his brain kept nagging, "I told you so. Cats never stay."

That night the temperature dropped, and although it seldom snowed heavily around Seattle, enough of the white stuff piled up on the ground to cause Kimberly additional concern for Elvira.

"Elvira will freeze to death, Daddy," she said, fighting back her tears the next afternoon when she came home from elementary school. "We have to go find her."

Harding knew locating a straying cat would be no small job in their area, which was still in the process of being transformed from farms and orchards to houses and yards. A number of rapidly deteriorating barns and outbuildings stood around the area. Elvira could be holed up in any of a hundred places—or she could have been killed by traffic, an unleashed dog, or one of the raccoons that stubbornly hung on to their rapidly vanishing turf.

"Please, Daddy, we have to go out and look for Elvira!"

Karen saw to it that they were both well bundled against the cold, and father and daughter set out in the gathering darkness in search of their missing cat.

In spite of Harding's pessimism, after about five minutes of Kimberly's plaintive calling, they seemed to hear answering meows from an old, falling-down barn.

Harding had to keep a firm grasp on his daughter's hand to stop her from running on ahead. He could not risk her stumbling over snow-covered debris or stepping on a rusty nail.

When the two of them finally found Elvira, it was hard to tell which of them was more amazed. The black cat had wrapped her furry self around the half-naked body of a very small baby girl.

"See, Daddy," Kimberly said, smiling through her tears of joy. "Elvira wasn't being naughty by staying out all night. She was taking care of the baby!"

The doctors at a nearby clinic agreed that the deathly pale baby would surely have frozen without the cat's constant attention. The abandoned child, only a few months old, had been kept alive by Elvira's body heat and by her vigorous licking. Thanks to the cat's intervention, "Baby Doe" would recover without any complications.

"Elvira is a hero, isn't she, Daddy?" Kimberly asked on the way home from the clinic, as she hugged the purring cat close. "She couldn't come home if she was going to save the baby girl's life!"

Harding agreed that Elvira must be forgiven for staying out all night without checking in. "Elvira is a hero," he repeated.

from CAT CAUGHT MY HEART

Private Smith's Joey

LYNN SEELY

lthough visiting the elderly was still new to me, I had already discovered some nursing homes were a place of solace—and some were not. The nursing home I was in route to this morning had clean, bright rooms as well as a staff that was considerate and cheerful. Even so, the elderly inhabitants are quite aware they will never leave or live an independent life again. Depression and withdrawal are common—especially for the patients who end up forgotten by relatives who never bother to visit. Perhaps sadder still are the patients who have outlived all their loved ones.

After parking my car I made my way to the nurse in charge. She was expecting me and had selected a patient who might benefit the most from a visit. "His name is Robert Smith and no one ever comes to visit him. Don't expect him to respond to you, though. He hasn't spoken in months." She smiled encouragingly as she added, "But he will know you are there and maybe that will cheer him up a bit."

A few minutes later I was in his room, seated only a few feet from the bed Mr. Smith occupied. I said nothing at first. After a few minutes I moved slightly, causing the wooden chair to creak rather loudly. Even then he made no sign he knew I was there. He had once been a strong young man but now he was a pitifully-frail old man who couldn't even walk unaided. As I looked at him, I wasn't thinking about how the years had produced this cruel transformation. Nor was I focusing on how sad it was that he never had visitors. My concentration was wholly on the dilemma of how to engage him in conversation. If I were successful in that, then perhaps it would coax him out of his depression a bit. Perhaps it would lift his spirits for a little while.

I looked at his listless face. His eyes stared straight ahead, blank and lifeless, yet I sensed he had deep feelings coursing just beneath his mask of apathy. After a few minutes of uncomfortable silence, for some unfathomable reason, I blurted out, "Did you ever like dogs?" The odd question hung in the air, awkward and unanswered, for the longest time.

I was about to apologize and amend my question to something more normal, such as "Did you ever own a dog?" when I noticed tears forming in his eyes. A remarkable transformation was taking place in front of me. Slowly, Robert turned his face toward me and stared at me, seeing me for the first time. His frail voice wavered as he spoke. "Well, I never did care for dogs much, at least not before that night." With that said, he paused. I had no idea what he meant, but just the fact that he had spoken to me was a good sign. I didn't want to ruin this breakthrough by saying the wrong thing so I decided to wait and see if he wanted to comment further. As I waited, his shaking hand found the control panel to his bed and he pressed a button on it. It raised the head of his bed up a little so he could see me easier.

Then he began a story, a story that took both of us to another time and place and introduced me to a remarkable dog named Joey. A dog, as it turned out, that had saved his life during World War II.

Robert's face reflected deep emotions as he spoke. "It was the winter of 1944 during World War II and I was serving overseas. I had seen my best friend killed when he stepped on a land mine. I watched the horror happen as if in slow motion. It was awful. It was not too long after that I was separated from my platoon, at least from what was left of them. I recall on this particular night I had made my way toward where they should have been, but when I got there I saw the enemy had occupied the area. Under cover of darkness I slipped away and made my way back to the only cover I could find—back to a house that had been bombed. It was all that was left that might provide cover for me.

"Soon after I reached it, I fell through the floor and down into what used to be the basement. I landed hard, the fall injured my leg and I suspected it was broken. I couldn't walk on it at all. I realized I was stranded behind the enemy line. It didn't look good at that point. Not good at all. I was only nineteen years old at the time, and it was easy to imagine I would not live to see twenty. I was all alone—and I had seen too much. Too many lives lost. Too much death. And now here I was, injured and in enemy territory, with little food and no way to stay warm. In that dark time, during that long night, I decided it might be easier to just allow the cold to numb my mind and body and just quit. I was ready to give up. It's a hard thing to admit even now, but I didn't want to go on.

"As I lay there in the dark, I decided to say a little prayer. I spoke quietly, barely above a whisper, and I asked for help. Then I made my peace with God. That night, I didn't expect I'd see the sunrise the next morning. Just after I finished praying, I heard a noise. I didn't even want to breathe, I was so scared. My heart was pounding so loud I thought the enemy could hear it. It was eerie, waiting for the next moment, for the next noise. I suddenly realized something. I didn't want to die after all. Under any circumstances.

"Then I heard the noise again. It was closer. It sounded like someone walking toward me. I pulled my gun up and got ready to fire. Then it occurred to me that it was possible it might not be the enemy. Maybe it was another American."

Robert paused for a moment before he went on. "I took a deep breath, then whispered, 'Who is it?'"

"Well, nothing happened for a moment, then I heard an answer. Sort of a whine or something. It sounded like a dog had answered me, and what struck me about it was that he had answered me as quiet as I had spoken.

"I snapped my fingers quietly, and the next thing I knew a large dog was beside me. He lay down next to me after licking my face once. He seemed exhausted and when I reached down to pet him, I realized he was extremely dirty. I could feel a collar around his neck and could tell he had a tag on it, but I couldn't risk striking a match to see what it said.

"Although I had never really cared much for dogs one way or an-

other, I found it comforting to have the dog next to me. His body gave off a lot of warmth and I started feeling warmer for the first time in hours. We spent the night that way, next to each other. We made it through the long night together. I did see the sunrise that morning. At first light I was able to inspect the dog and read his tag. His name was Joey. He was a large dog, solid black in color. That morning we were able to look each other in the eye. His solemn gaze told me a lot. I had the feeling we had both lost friends recently. I said to him, 'Seems we're both in a mess, aren't we, boy?' Joey looked up at me and answered with a brief wave of his tail.

"Well, that day, and for the next few days, I could hear the troops and enemy vehicles close by. At one point it occurred to me that I would be as good as dead if Joey barked at them. But he never did.

"The pain in my leg was pretty bad, but as long as I didn't move, it was tolerable. I had two major concerns. The first was that I might be discovered. I figured they would probably shoot me. The second problem was food and water. I only had a small amount of both."

Robert's eyes were bright as he continued. "Well, the first day Joey was with me, we just stayed put. But the next day, when I woke up at first light, I found out the dog was gone. I figured he had run off. And I sure couldn't blame him, though I missed him a lot. In fact, I missed him more than a lot. And I worried about him, too. Well, just a few minutes after I woke up, I noticed something right next to me. An egg. Now that was a little strange. Had a chicken come up next to me and laid an egg? That was just too preposterous a notion, yet the egg was there. I picked it up and ate it.

"But not the shell. I didn't eat that," Robert clarified. "Anyway, just about that time, here comes Joey. Boy, was I glad to see him! Well, he walks right over to me and he lowers his head almost to the ground and he drops something—an egg! Then he looks up at me and waves his tail real slow. Like he was waiting for me to say something.

"Now I figure this is one smart dog, but even more than that, this is one very unselfish dog. I mean, here he was bringing food to me when he could have gobbled it all up himself."

Robert stopped talking for a moment as he reminisced about Joey. "You know," he began again, "that dog did that every day, just before dawn. Some days he would bring me one egg, and some days he would make several trips and bring me two or three eggs. And when I would offer one to him, he would refuse. I figured he must have been eating his eggs at the place where he was getting them, and then he'd carefully bring some back to me. He never did break any.

"Joey was successful at not getting caught and at preventing me from starving. He never deserted me. We stayed like that for almost two weeks. Right smack under the enemy's nose. And they never knew! I'd like to think that Joey was stealing the eggs from the enemy, but I don't see how he could have. He probably got them from some farm somewhere. No matter where he got them from, one thing for sure is that he saved my life."

Robert was smiling now, his face clearly communicating the pride he felt about Joey. "The allies finally pushed the enemy back and we were finally rescued. You know, I never did find out who Joey had belonged to. There wasn't any record of him anywhere. And I got to keep him. He returned with me to the States and lived a long happy life with me. He was the smartest dog I ever saw. I mean, he had real intelligence. Joey lived with me over ten years before he died." Tears formed in

Robert's eyes before he added, "But Joey had a legacy, you know. He fathered puppies with a dog that belonged to a good friend of mine. We each kept a pup from that litter. And Joey was great with that puppy, too. He showed him the ropes and taught that puppy everything he could.

"I have a picture of Joey." With that, Robert pulled a tattered old photo from his shirt pocket and thrust it at me. I took it and looked into the face of a gentle giant of a dog. I smiled at Robert, then looked back at the photo. Joey looked just as I had pictured him in my mind. I returned the picture to Robert. He gazed at it for a moment and then carefully placed it in his pocket.

Robert fell quiet, yet it was a comfortable silence this time, a silence shared by two friends. I was so grateful that he had shown me Joey's picture and shared his inspiring story. I finally broke the silence and whispered one heartfelt word: "Thanks." As I spoke Robert reached over, grabbed my hand, squeezed it gently for a moment; then, with a contented sigh, he leaned back and closed his eyes. He was tired. It was time for me to go. I eased quietly out of my chair and tiptoed to the door. I was already looking forward to my next visit with him.

I could tell he was pleased that he had shared his story about his remarkable dog. And that in doing so, for a short time, he was able to be with his beloved Joey again.

When I returned the following week to visit Robert, I learned that he had passed away a few days earlier. The nurse told me that he died peacefully in his sleep. She turned to go, then turned back to me and added, "You know, when Robert was found, he was clutching an old faded photo of a large black dog. There wasn't any writing on the photo, so we don't know any more about the picture. I suppose that may have been the last thing he saw before he went to sleep."

I didn't say anything to her that day. I would tell her what I knew about the picture another time when I was better composed and didn't have a lump in my throat. I left the nursing home, saddened by the news of Robert's death. Yet I did take a little comfort in the thought that perhaps—just perhaps—Robert Smith and his beloved Joey were together again.

A Healing Touch

Restore to me the joy

of thy salvation, and uphold me

with a willing spirit

(Psalm 51:12, RSV).

The Unseen Bird

MARY ALICE BAUMGARDNER

ravel crunched under my sandals as I walked down the lane. A gentle breeze challenged the heat of the summer sun. I needed to walk. I needed to be alone.

Two months earlier, on June 8, 1998, an automobile accident claimed the life of my youngest son, Michael. No mother ever expects to survive her child. It never occurred to me that Michael and his hopes and dreams would be buried before his twenty-first birthday.

I loved and trusted our heavenly Father. Psalm 139 had comforted me and reassured me that God knows before we are born the number of days we shall live. On that fateful day, Michael could have died in his sleep or choked to death on a chicken bone. Instead, a friend, driving too fast on a winding country road, skidded, lost control of the car, and crashed backwards into a tree. He watched helplessly, unable to rescue Michael, as flames engulfed the automobile. We were told that our son died instantly: his aorta burst on impact. My heart had broken, too. But I remained on earth.

I continued walking down the lane. More than anything I wanted to hug my Mikey again. More than anything, I wanted to tell him how much I loved him. My throat tightened. I blinked back tears.

As I approached the middle of the tree-lined lane, I heard a beautiful melody. Intrigued, I tried to catch a glimpse of the songster. I wanted to be able to identify him. As the unseen bird warbled loudly, I circled the tree. Then, for a long time, I stood still...waiting, watching, and listening. I never did see the bird.

However, even though I didn't see that bird, I knew that he was very much alive. Suddenly I realized that so it is, too, with my Michael. Even though I can no longer see him or hug him, he is also very much alive. I felt his presence there—exuberant and joyful. It was as if he said, "I'm okay, Mom. This is fantastic!"

In 2 Corinthians 4:18 (TEV), Saint Paul writes: "For we fix our attention, not on things that are seen, but on things that are unseen. What can be seen lasts only for a time, but what cannot be seen lasts forever." A little unseen bird reminded me of that truth.

I became numb after Michael's accident. I had loved writing and illustrating children's books. I could not write. I could not draw. I thought perhaps I could paint in oils. I thought they might offer a sort of therapy, I guess. No paintings ever resulted from my efforts. I had no interest in doing anything.

But, nonetheless, thoughts came to me. I called them "musings." It was through very brief "musings" that I was able to express what I felt during those months when I was still so numb. Words slipped into my heart, needing to be written. One of the first "musings" was what I learned from the little unseen bird:

> A lovely, lilting melody
> enchanted me
> as I walked along the lane.
> Stretching on tiptoe,
> encircling the tree,
> I tried to see the tiny songster.
>
> Sunshine splashed gold
> upon my face.

Shadows danced
with the breeze.
And though thick foliage
hid the little bird,
it could not hide his song.

There is a veil that
separates us, too,
since you have gone.
But, like that little unseen bird,
I still can hear
your song.

A Miracle Named Munchie

THIRZA PEEVEY

I made it to the shower and turned the water on full blast before I started crying. My roommates didn't need to know that I was crying. I didn't want to depress them.

I just didn't know what else to do for my friend, Frances. I was totally at a loss and so were her doctors. Three months ago, she had the flu. She thought the cats must have been sleeping on her feet while she was sick, but the tingly, painful sensation didn't go away. Instead it began creeping up her legs. It moved on to her hands and arms. It kept steadily creeping upward.

Her doctors were perplexed at first, but after a spinal tap they offered up the diagnosis of Guillaume-Barre syndrome. "It's a rare disease," they told me. "Actually we've never seen it before. There really isn't anything we can do for her except give her pain killers. She doesn't have health insurance, so we are going to let you take her home and watch her. If the paralysis gets to her chest she will die, and there is nothing we can do. We wouldn't be able to do much even if she were here in the hospital. If she makes it to Monday, we will do another spinal tap and see if it is advancing or retreating."

Frances had made it to Monday, and in fact the paralysis had started reversing so she refused the second spinal tap. That was when the real trial started. As the paralysis had moved forward, it had damaged and even killed many nerve cells. At least, that was the explanation offered at the time. As it reversed, the nerve cells started to heal and regenerate. That was when the severe pain began. Most of the time, the pain killers barely dulled the pain. She sat in her bed and shook with the intensity of it and bit her lip until it bled to keep from screaming. She said she felt as if her arms and legs were on fire. Her feet felt as if the bones were coming through the skin. Lord only knows what mixed-up messages her brain was getting from the damaged nerve cells.

Frances' husband was starting a new business and couldn't be in both places at once, so I tried to help every way I could. I came every night after work and took care of her seven cats, three dogs and one rabbit. I changed her bed and got her something to eat. I tidied the house and vacuumed. I did the laundry and the dishes. I set out drinks, snacks and medicine for the next day and made sure she had the TV remote and things to read, because she was trapped in bed and couldn't walk. But I couldn't stop the soul-destroying pain. Nothing touched it. So every night I took care of her needs and tucked her into bed and then I went home and stood in the shower and cried.

The months passed and the pain continued. By sheer grit, Frances was regaining the use of her arms and legs. True to her cantankerous nature, she began crawling around the house on her hands and knees to do housework. Some days I arrived to find her pants soaked in blood around the knees from crawling until her knees blistered and the blisters broke. That made it better somehow for her because she didn't feel as helpless, but it made me feel terrible. Time and time again we squabbled over staying in bed so her body could heal. Actually, I squabbled. She looked away and refused to listen.

Within a few weeks, Frances discovered that one leg was strong enough to support her. The other could support her weight from the knee up, but the foot and lower leg were too weak. She overcame this difficulty by taking a lightweight side chair and using it as a peg leg. She would kneel on the chair with the weak leg while she swung the

115

strong one forward. Then, standing on the strong leg, she pulled the chair and the weak leg forward. In this unorthodox fashion she began getting around the house to dust, cook and vacuum. Soon she was taking care of everything but the laundry and the cat pans. That made her feel a little less helpless and bored, but the crushing pain and the feeling of being trapped remained. We still didn't know if it was ever going to get better.

Spring arrived, and with it, her favorite time of year. She was walking now, but her left leg was not much bigger around than the bone itself. All the muscle had wasted away. Her balance was severely affected by the lack of strength on that side and she couldn't trust herself on uneven ground.. She was trapped indoors and could only watch spring unfold through the window. I think that was almost harder for her than all the rest of the indignities of being sick. Her orneriness had kept her going so far, but I wondered how long she could cope with being unable to do the things she loved. Then one weekend, she pounced.

As I came in to the house she ordered me, "Go get Munchie. Harness her up and put her to the work cart. Meet me outside the garage in half an hour." I was a bit startled, to say the least. Munchie was her little white Welsh pony. Purchased for her daughter fifteen years before, Farnley Keepsake had proved to be a bit too much pony for a child. She had repeatedly bucked the child off and had galloped off with her tail flipped over her back. Something about her ornery nature had appealed to Frances, however, and the two had bonded. Frances broke the pony to drive a cart. Christened "Munchkin or Munchie," she became a local star at carriage driving shows. Soon the interior walls of both garages were covered with ribbons that Frances and Munchie had won. I had shown against Munchie, however, and I knew what a handful that pony could be. There was no way Frances could drive the pony in her current condition, even in an indoor arena, and I told her so.

"Listen," Frances replied, "I have been driving that pony over the same route every day for fifteen years. She knows the route. She knows to look both ways before pulling out into traffic. She knows to wait while I open the gate to the practice field. She can drive our route without me. Get the pony, I'm going driving."

I suppose I could have said no. In Frances' current condition there wasn't much she could have done about it, but something told me it would break her spirit if I did. I went and got the pony. "Besides," I thought to myself as I groomed the pony and harnessed her, "I'll be there to help if anything goes wrong." When I finished preparing the pony, I helped Frances out the door and supported her as she sat on the seat and pivoted into the cart. I started to step into the cart myself, but she picked up the whip and shook it at me.

"Now you go away," she said. "I'll be back in an hour and I'll need you to help me out of the cart and put the pony away."

Well, what else was I going to do? I let her go. I watched the pony trot to the end of the lane and wait for traffic to clear. Then she turned left into the road, carefully leaving enough room for the cart to clear the farm signboard so that the wheels wouldn't catch. I went in the house and started my chores, frantically checking the windows every few minutes and listening for the sounds of hooves on the road. An hour later I was relieved to hear slow clip-clopping as Munchie walked in the driveway. I hurried downstairs to help Frances out of the cart and put the pony away.

Frances was radiant. "I got to forget, just for a little while, about the pain and about being sick. For a little while I got to be alone and not have anyone fussing over me. I got to just be me. But now my feet are freezing—get me in the house, please."

Ever patient, Munchie stood quietly outside the garage until I had Frances settled in a chair upstairs. Then I came downstairs, unhooked her and put the harness away. I gave her a good brushing and took her to the barn. "You are some pony, old girl," I whispered into her tiny white ears. "I think you may have found a way to give us all hope."

A few weeks later, Munchie showed me that she really did know how to drive herself, and I really didn't need to worry about them in traffic. I heard Munchie coming in the driveway and went out to meet her as usual. Frances wasn't in the cart. "Where did you leave Mom, old girl?" I asked her. I was just about to get in the cart and go looking when I saw Frances jogging down the driveway. When she caught her breath, she told me what had happened.

"When I closed the gate at Hathaway's, I tripped and stumbled against the cart. Munchie thought I'd gotten in and started up the hill. I tried to catch her, but I wasn't quick enough. She paused at the top of the hill, looked both ways and turned on to the right side of the road. She walked the first few paces, as I'd taught her, and then broke into a trot just as if I was in the carriage. I almost caught her, but I was a split second too slow. At the end of the street, she stopped for the stop sign and waited for traffic to clear. As heavy as traffic is on Caves Road, I almost caught up to her again, but she got a break in the traffic and turned right toward home, being careful to leave enough clearance so the hub wouldn't catch the stop sign. She stayed on the right side near the shoulder and trotted all the way to our lane, then turned right into the driveway, again leaving clearance for the signboard. She came right to the garage door and stopped for me to get out."

"I know," I replied. "She couldn't understand where you were. She kept looking around, trying to find you."

After that, I never worried about them being out alone together. Munchie really could drive herself and, thanks to that little incident,

I knew that Frances was now strong enough to walk home if need be. Frances drove her almost every day and began feeling more like herself and less like a patient. Walking to and from the cart, opening the gate at Hathaway's all forced her to walk independently and built strength back in her legs. Holding the reins forced her to use her hands and arms and rebuilt strength there, too. Most of all, it lifted her spirits.

Before long, Frances could get the pony from the barn by herself and wasn't dependent on me or my schedule anymore. Through the summer she grew stronger and stronger. Within a year of the onset of the illness, she was nearly back to normal, except for one cold foot. I suppose that she would have mended without the pony, but I still believe the turning point came when Munchie gave her something to look forward to each day. That was when Frances began to believe she would make it. And she did.

Companion Pieces

CHRISTINE HERMAN MERRILL

s long as I can remember, I've loved animals. As soon as I could walk, I'd scatter bread crumbs in the yard, then sit on my mother's lap and watch the animals eat. How I loved the silly, scampering squirrels, the bossy bluejays and timid sparrows.

When I was three, a majestic white cat showed up at our back door, and my mother let me keep him—much to the dismay of our neighborhood birds and squirrels, who became the object of his many hunting expeditions. But what a gentle creature he was with the family! His noble demeanor remained unchanged even when I picked him up by the throat or cut off all his long whiskers with Mother's scissors.

I suppose my becoming an artist was predestined. My mother was an artist, and her mother, and her mother before her. When I was two, my mother put a pencil in my hand, and I immediately started drawing animals. By the time I was in grade school, I knew I wanted to combine my talent for drawing with my love of animals to make animal portraiture my career.

When I was seven, I decided I wanted a dog. I had read all about dogs in the *1968 Encyclopædia Britannica* my father had bought, and had carefully scrutinized the photos of the various breeds. I wanted either a Pekingese or a Pomeranian. I begged. I pleaded. I cried. I drew countless pictures of dogs and plastered them all over the house as little reminders. I swore the puppy would be no trouble to my parents. That fall, when I fell off my bike and bloodied my mouth, my father presented me with a beagle—a stuffed one. I cried.

Four days before my eighth birthday, I was drawing in the sun parlor when I heard my father's car pull up. He was home early from work. I ran to the front window. There he was, getting out of his car in his rumpled gray raincoat, when he reached back in and picked up something tiny and black.

"Dad's home, and it looks like he's brought you another stuffed toy," my older sister, Eleanor, called to me from upstairs.

"No, it's not!" I cried. "It's a real dog!"

Dad came in wearing a broad grin and placed the puppy on the floor. He was so small and wobbly he could hardly stand. I named him Pom Pom the Pomeranian.

As Mother instructed, we put him in a towel-lined box in the kitchen that night. But his high-pitched wails broke my heart. I sneaked downstairs and brought him up to my bed, where he slept every night for the next eighteen years.

I was true to my word and cared for Pom Pom myself. I fed him, washed and brushed him, walked him. My eighth birthday fell on Easter, and Mother had the house brightly decorated with Easter baskets, Easter bunnies, and dyed eggs. I couldn't resist putting Pom Pom in an Easter basket centerpiece with yellow stuffing and colored eggs. So sweet and gentle, the Easter puppy just stayed there.

In September my parents separated, and a bitter divorce process began. Whenever I was sad or crying, Pom Pom would always come and nudge his nose under my hand and gaze at me with eyes as moist as mine. Sometimes, just to get away from the sadness of the house, I would give him rides in the deep basket of my bicycle. He loved to race into the wind, ears back, nose up, sniffing the scents of the neighborhood.

In my spare time I drew and painted Pom Pom in dozens of positions—in pencil, charcoal, oils. "Sleeping Pom Pom," "Frisky Pom Pom," "Wistful Pom Pom." It was easiest to sketch him when he was in a sound sleep. I would sit cross-legged, sketching him, then turn over a new page, move a few feet around him, and start a new sketch. Sometimes I even stood over him and sketched the aerial view.

I had always liked to sketch animals in unexpected positions, instead of the standard frontal view. I often sketched Pom Pom from behind, his head bent around looking back at me. By the time he was two, he had grown thick, white puffs on his hindquarters that almost trailed on the ground, and his curly, upturned tail sprouted long gray hair. I started experimenting with charcoal, to duplicate the rich range of grays. And through these early sketches of Pom Pom I tried to capture an animal's soul—roguish or relaxed, noble or playful.

When Pom Pom was twelve, I painted an oval oil portrait of him. His muzzle was tinged with white, which gave him a distinguished look. His brown eyes sparkled with compassion. Then I painted a self-portrait with Pom Pom in my arms. It hangs on my wall now. Sometimes I laugh when I look at it. Such a serious portrait, and the composition reminds me of a Madonna and Child. Since then, I have always enjoyed painting animals with their keepers, to show the close relationship between them.

When I left my childhood home for a house of my own, Pom Pom came with me. Toward the end, he couldn't see or hear very well and didn't walk around much, but he always seemed content. I coaxed him to eat and carried him from room to room so he could always be near me. One evening he passed away in his sleep, a painless ending so suited to his gentle soul.

Pom Pom lives in my paintings, in every pair of shining brown eyes I paint, in the curve of a tail, in the turn of a head. My mother taught me to paint, but if I am able to capture on canvas a dog's unique personality, his devotion, his warmth and joy, it's because of what Pom Pom taught me—the spiritual bond between a dog and a human family.

from DOG PEOPLE

The Aquarium in Our Living Room

RUBY BAYAN

As far back as I can remember there had always been an aquarium on the built-in hardwood divider shelf that separated the dining room from the living room in our old house. The five-gallon aquarium fit snugly into the divider as if the shelf was specifically built around it.

My earliest recollection this aquarium was when I was too small to reach the top of the tank, and I would climb up the arm of the couch beside the shelf to take an active part in feeding our colorful swimming pets. Somehow, in my youth, I considered the aquarium a basic element in our house, and feeding the fish an integral part of our family's daily routine. On some weekends, I would watch my mother clean out the tank, meticulously re-landscape and re-decorate the habitat, and re-stock the tank by bringing in the most colorful tropical fishes.

We had a backyard pond that had some wild guppies and exotic swordtails, and my mother would pick out the best ones to put in our living room aquarium. This was the life I was born into, so the aquarium and the tropical fish just seemed to belong in our regular scheme of things.

123

In our pre-school years, my brother and I would constantly be attracted to the tank, and, of course, naughty as we were, we'd drop anything and everything into it to see how the fish would react or just to find out how our innovative underwater décor would look. A few shiny marbles would be okay, but most of the time my mother would sigh in exasperation when she had to rescue various items from the bottom of the tank, such as the flashlight we thought would remain lit underwater, the alarm clock that looked art nouveau half-buried in the sand, and, of course, the multi-colored crayons.

Patiently, my mother would tell us why these items did not belong inside the aquarium. "They are harmful to the fish because they pollute the water and disturb the balance," she would say, trying her best to make our innocent minds comprehend.

Eventually, we understood that we couldn't drop our stuff into the water, so my brother and I resorted to "interacting" with the fish instead. We would splash the water and tap the walls of the tank.

"No, kids, don't tap the glass because the fishes feel the pounding in their ears!" my mother warned us, emphasizing that the fish could hear our voices through the water, and they got hurt when we tapped the glass. I didn't pay much attention to what my mother was actually saying then. But I soon realized that she had been teaching my brother and me our first lessons in being kind to animals.

Over the years, the family aquarium continued to evolve, and the various fish inhabitants came and went. But there was never a time when we didn't have a bustling community of fishes that my mother would lovingly attend to every single day.

It was only when I was about ready to move out of our old home to live in a place of my own that I took the time to ask my mother the question I had always wanted to ask her. "Mom, we've cared for dogs, cats, rabbits, and hamsters, but none of them became a constant in our lives like these fishes in this aquarium. Why is that?"

My mother eagerly answered, "Fishes in an aquarium are probably the easiest pets to take care of. You don't have to housetrain them, take them out for a walk, or bring them to the groomers. They don't give you allergies, and they don't keep you up at night.

"Instead, a thriving community of fishes in an aquarium move about gracefully, and give you soothing performances of astounding

124

hues and colors, and smooth and agile motions in a world of harmony and indescribable charm." I told her I wasn't sure I totally understood what she meant, but she was glad to explain.

"The fishes are my escape when life gets a bit harsh and unbearable," she said. "I just sit and watch them and blend into their tranquility and balance. They help me relax."

My mother then uttered what may have completely influenced my perception of tropical fish for the rest of my life. She said, "Very soon you will start your own family and live your own life. Remember what I told you about the fishes—they will help you maintain your sanity. They will give you peace. Let them do this for you as they have done for me."

I understood. And I remembered.

The Girls

BARBARA A. SEITZ

eeling a little depressed, I decided to do something about it. For along time I had been thinking how much fun it would be to have a kitten. After giving this much thought, I decided I wanted to have two. The reason for wanting two, was so they would always have each other for company and would never be lonesome. One day a friend of mine called and told me about a woman who had two Persian kittens. She said they were sisters and I should go see them before someone else did. My life was about to change.

I called at once and made an appointment for the next morning. When I arrived, they both were in a large cage, playing with each other. They were three months old and had just had a bath. One look and I knew they would be going home with me. I did not know which one was cuter. One was silver-gray and the other black. They were night and day, as opposite as salt and pepper. Both came running over to me and I fell in love instantly. When I left that day, they were right beside me. It would be a decision that I never regretted.

When I woke up the following morning and found both of them cuddled up next to me, my depression vanished. I could not wait to get up each day to watch their antics. Their personalities were as contrasting as their colors. I named them Tiffany and Chanel. Chanel was more independent and appeared stronger in all ways. Tiffany had to control everything! If they fought over a toy or favorite spot to sleep, Tiffany always won. Chanel would get annoyed and go off by herself. When Tiffany was afraid of anything, she would hide behind Chanel for protection.

Both adjusted to their new surroundings immediately. It was a big house and together they explored every nook and cranny. I never knew where I would find them. Everything they did, they did together. The two ate from the same dishes. Sometimes Tiffany would sit in front of the food, glare at Chanel, and not let her eat. Chanel would sadly stare back, sit and wait. She knew Tiffany would soon get bored and look for something more exciting to do. The two would playfully fight, but seldom got into anything serious.

My sister gave them a cat video. It had birds and squirrels in it and they loved it. Chanel would sit very still and watch closely. Tiffany would crouch down and growl at it. Whatever they were doing, if I called and said, "Come watch your video," they would come running. Tiffany loved a commercial on television about a ceiling fan. She would watch intently, then would keep looking up at the ceiling, watching our fan. I had never realized how intelligent cats really were. Every day was a new experience with them, a new awakening.

That year I started my flower seeds indoors. Other years I had tried, without much success. I could not believe I finally managed to accomplish it. They were full, a deep green, and very healthy looking. I removed the cover and placed them in a bay window, so they would have the sunlight. Running to the phone, I called my sister to tell her the good news. When we hung up, I went back to the window to admire my seedlings and could not believe what I was seeing. Tiffany and Chanel were standing in the window looking at me. They had eaten the top off each plant. After the initial shock, I laughed. I could not get mad at them and they knew it.

Both were house cats and afraid of certain things. The two did not like strangers, so I bathed them myself. Both Tiffany and Chanel liked the hair dryer. I combed them every day and they loved it. Their coats were as delicate as the finest silk, as soft as cotton. I never grew tired of the extra work involved. To me they were worth every moment of it. It meant I had to vacuum every day and I gladly did so. I considered myself fortunate for having such pleasure in my life. No matter what happened during the day, they could always bring a smile to my face.

Both were very gentle by nature. Occasionally they would find a bug walking around. This was a big event in their life. Both would sit, practically on top of it, and watch every move it made. If it stopped walking, they would gently push it until it moved again, never hurting it. Twice they caught a mouse. After they caught it, they would let it go, and then try to catch it again. Although they were house cats, they were quick, strong, and alert.

When I did the grocery shopping, I would buy them a present. Of course they knew this and would sit patiently waiting as I emptied the bags. Sometimes they liked their gifts and would play with them for a long time. Other times, they took an instant dislike to something and would sulk. They were disappointed and wanted to make sure I was aware of this. Whatever their reaction was, it would make me laugh. If Tiffany did not like the food I gave her, she would glare at me. She knew I would replace it with something she liked better. Chanel was not as particular. She would eat most anything put in front of her.

When Tiffany and Chanel were four years old, both started to have health problems. It was the beginning of a long round of visits to the veterinarians. They prescribed different medications but nothing seemed to work. One doctor taught me how to give them medicine by tilting their heads back. This always worked for her, but never for me. Finally, I tried giving it to them on a teaspoon and they liked that much better. It was so easy!

Sadly, the medicine didn't work, and the day came when I knew they would have to put my beloved companions to sleep. This news was heartrending. How could I accept that I would lose both? Yet I do not think that losing one would have been any easier. The one thing that gave me comfort was that they would be together. Tiffany and Chanel had never been apart in life. Now they would spend an eternity with each other.

Saying goodbye was hard, but they will live forever in my heart. I know they crossed that place called "The Rainbow Bridge" and are patiently waiting for me. We will meet again. *This I know.*

The Power of Love

MARY M. ALWARD

elly came to us on a rainy autumn day in the late 60's. As Lisa descended the steps of the school bus, she heard whimpers of distress. She searched the area and finally found Kelly hiding in the culvert at the end of the driveway. She picked up the thin, shivering pup and brought her to the house, wrapped in her jacket.

When I first saw Kelly, I was horrified. Her tiny body was thin; her ribs could be seen pushing at her skin. Her stomach was swollen from lack of nourishment. Her head drooped. She was lethargic and every time she was moved, she whimpered in pain.

Aunt Millie immediately took a liking to the half-starved pup. She warmed some milk on the old woodstove, put it in a dish and set it before the trembling ball of fur. The pup struggled to lift her head but soon gave up, flopping onto her side. Aunt Millie searched frantically in the medicine chest until she found an old glass eyedropper. She cuddled the pup in her arms and gently coaxed her to swallow the milk that she dropped into her mouth.

No one held much hope for the pup's survival. Uncle Jim said if she lasted the night it would be a miracle. Aunt Millie, who'd always had a soft spot for animals, was determined to save the pup's life. She sat up all night in her oak rocker, holding the dog in her arms. She stroked its fine red hair and crooned to it lovingly. When dawn turned the eastern sky to hues of pink, purple and blue, Aunt Millie was fast asleep in her rocker. The Red Setter pup slept soundly on her lap.

As soon as Lisa was safely on the school bus that morning, Aunt Millie put the pup, which she'd named Kelly because it was "a good old Irish name," into the old, rusty pickup truck and headed for town. Kelly was going to the vet's.

The vet examined Kelly thoroughly and told Aunt Millie that Kelly was suffering from exposure. If she received lots of nourishment and love, she would be fine. That was all Aunt Millie needed to hear. She spent hours cuddling, petting and talking to Kelly. Within a few days, the dog was following her around the kitchen. Within a month, Kelly looked like any other Red Setter pup. She had a flamboyant personality and her antics sent the entire family into fits of laughter.

Kelly and Stripe, the barn cat, also formed a firm bond. They played and tumbled in the yard and soon had become good friends. But Kelly's first love was Aunt Millie and the feeling was mutual. Aunt Millie adored the beautiful Red Setter.

As Kelly grew, the bond between her and Aunt Millie became firmer. When Aunt Millie went to town, Kelly would whimper and whine until she returned. Kelly always knew when Aunt Millie was coming. She would hear the pickup coming down the road and would run down the driveway full-tilt to meet the truck at the end of the lane. Aunt Millie always kept a sharp eye out for Kelly, who would race alongside the truck, barking furiously, until it reached the driveshed.

One day when Kelly was two years old, she heard the pickup coming from town. She raced down the lane to meet it. This time Aunt Millie wasn't driving. Hank, the hired hand, turned into the driveway, making a wide turn. The front bumper of the truck collided with Kelly's left hip. Her lovely red body tumbled beneath the wheels.

Uncle Jim wrapped Kelly in a blanket and rushed her to the vet. Her left rear leg was severely mangled. The vet said amputation was Kelly's only hope; pins and splints would be of no avail. Kelly's leg would never heal. After much discussion between Uncle Jim and Aunt Millie, surgery to amputate Kelly's leg was underway.

It didn't take Kelly's leg long to heal. She was young, healthy and strong. Within a few days, much to our surprise, she was beginning to adapt to her disability. She was confined to the kitchen, but in spite of this was in great spirits. She did her best to follow Aunt Millie as she cooked and cleaned.

Within two months, Kelly was her old self again. She raced down the lane on three legs almost as fast as she had on four. We were amazed at the strength she showed.

For five years Kelly lived a normal life, doing all the things farm dogs do. She brought the cattle to the barn at milking time, chased Stripe and the squirrels around the yard and played fetch with Aunt Millie and Lisa.

When Kelly was six, tragedy struck once more. Her mobility began to decrease and in the beginning, we all assumed her old injury was being effected by arthritis. It wasn't long until her right rear leg that had always compensated for the disability began to swell. She began to lie around most of the day. When she did move, she'd whine and whimper with pain.

After trying everything she could think of, Aunt Millie decided to take Kelly to the vet. The news wasn't good. He took a biopsy. It came back positive. Kelly had cancer. It was possible that surgery would save her life but it would be costly and he offered no guarantees.

That afternoon I found Aunt Millie sitting in her rocker, her fingers lovingly caressing the fan quilt that my great-grandmother had given her on her wedding day. The quilt had been in the family for generations and was considered an heirloom.

"I'm going to sell it to Mrs. Cassidy," Aunt Millie said, her voice trembling. "She's wanted it for years. The money will pay for Kelly's vet bills."

Later that day I went with Aunt Millie to Mrs. Cassidy's antique shop. As I watched, I realized how hard it was for my aunt to relinquish the quilt. She took the money and drove straight to the vet's.

Kelly came through the surgery with flying colors, but the effects from the chemotherapy she was subjected to over the next few weeks left her listless and lethargic. We often wondered if she would make it.

As Kelly recuperated, Aunt Millie spent hours sitting on the floor with the dog's head in her lap. She would stroke Kelly and gently croon to her as she'd done that day so long ago when Lisa first brought her home. Within three months, Kelly was once again frolicking in the yard with Stripe and following Aunt Millie around the farm. Even the vet was amazed at her ability to overcome obstacles.

Never underestimate the power of love. It sustained Kelly through the major tragedies of her life. She died in her sleep six years later in her favorite spot—on the rag rug beside Aunt Millie's bed.

A few years later, as Aunt Millie lay in her bedroom dying of the cancer that was slowly devouring her body, her mind wandered back in time. She often reached over the side of the bed and stroked Kelly's head. The doctors and nurses said she was delirious. I doubted it. I believe that somehow Kelly was able to return to Aunt Millie in her final days to help her make the transition from life to death. The power of love is amazing.

Finding
the Way Home

Now I am sending him home again,

for he has been homesick

for all of you...

(Philippians 2:25, LB).

Mallard Fever

R. D. LARSON

y Grandpa had a ranch up in the hills. It was much bigger than our small farm. One time when he came to visit he brought me a pair of Mallard ducks. "These ducks joined my tame ducks, Rose," he told me. He set the box down. I looked inside and saw two beautiful ducks. One had a blue-and-green head and the other was a soft mottled brown. "They can be pets for you, since you're so crazy about animals. They're getting beat up by my ducks and they're too dumb to fly off."

Out of the corner of my eye, I could see my mother's lips parting. There was just the tiniest of frowns on her forehead. My dad pushed back his hat. Before they could say a word, I knelt at the box.

"Oh, I love them! I'm going to call him King Farouk and her Queen Ava. They're so beautiful."

"Baby, they're wild ducks. They'll most likely go off with other wild ducks," my mother said.

"No, Claire, don't think so, they've gotten used to eating grain and they stay close. If they went back to wild, they couldn't survive," said my grandfather, his eyes sparkling. Somehow he knew Mama was going to say that I couldn't keep the ducks. "Foxes would get 'em."

135

"But she already has a dog, a pony, three cats, two rabbits and a calf. Plus all our other animals. Dad, she brings all of them in the house!" Mama almost shrieked. She wasn't an animal person.

"Oh, honey, these aren't much bother," Pop said, because he loves animals same as me. "Besides, Rose hasn't been bringing in anything much but the dog and the cats. Oh—and that toad,"

"Take them outside now, Baby Rose. Then you scoot back in here to help with dinner," Mama said. She sort of wrinkled her nose at the duck smell.

I took them out and put them in the old chicken pen. But I could see they didn't like that. So I opened the gate and propped it with a board. I went to the barn with Farouk and Ava waddling right behind me. It was funny, like a parade.

I got some grain from the chicken feed barrel. When I knelt down and held it out in my hand, they took turns eating it. Their funny scooping bills nibbled and tickled. Once I felt Farouk's duck tongue— I did, really—just like he licked me. I loved them. They were so funny, waddling and making duck whispers, like tiny, low quacks. Farouk had only two toes on one foot. Maybe that's why they had gotten tame, I thought. He waddled with a limp.

Grandpa stayed the night and read to me out of the *National Geographic* about planes in England. That night before bed we had some of Mama's angel food cake and homemade raspberry sauce from our bushes.

"Girlie, you sure can cook," Grandpa told Mama when she dished him up a second helping. "I'll be sorry to be heading back home tomorrow. Sure is worth driving a hundred miles for your cooking."

"She's famous, huh, Dad?" My brother said.

"Yep, famous," my pop said and grinned at Mama. She looked so pretty with her chestnut hair all around her shoulders. "Everyone loves her cooking."

"Why, thank you, I'm so glad you like my angel cake," Mama said. She knew how to take compliments, being from the south and all. Then she gave my brother a never-before-that-I-could remember second helping. My brother, who is such a noodle, had gotten a pocketknife from Grandpa, one of his old ones, with only a tiny chip in the blade. I said I wanted some more cake, too.

"Well, I don't know—."

"Oh, Girlie, give the kid another piece of cake," Grandpa pleaded. I giggled. I never could have enough dessert. And she gave me another helping.

When I immediately got sick, Mama felt awful. "Oh, Baby, I shouldn't have let you have a second piece of cake. What was I thinking?"

"It tasted so good, Mama, thank you," I said to her. I hugged everyone, said goodnight and went to bed.

I went in my room off the kitchen and I could hear them talking about the ducks. I tried to listen but went to sleep without knowing it.

The next morning was Monday. All day I worried about my ducks. They were okay before I went to school and I'd left them water. I went to see them the minute I got off the bus. When I went into the house for my after-school snack. my mother said that we were driving into town.

Then she said that I should put Farouk and Ava into their box. I felt awful.

"We're going to take them to Sequoia Park and let them loose down at the duck pond. They'll like it there. Lots of bugs to eat. Baby Rose, stop now, those ducks can't live here. They're wild ducks," Mama told me, holding me. I would have none of it. My heart was breaking. I pulled away.

I was so sad and so mad that I rushed straight out of the house. I went to the barn to cry. And I prayed, too. Those were MY ducks. I stayed out there as long as I could.

But the deed had to be done. The eight miles to the park was like walking down death row. When we got to the park, Mama helped me set the cardboard box down by the duck pond. Farouk looked at me and looked at all the other ducks. Ava just sat down in the box. I think she was afraid of all those stranger ducks that she didn't know.

I couldn't say a word for the tears that choked me. I rode home, thinking. As soon as the car the stopped I went to start my chores. I fed the chickens. They seemed so unfriendly after Farouk and Ava. I fed the rabbits and brought in the eggs. Finally, I lay in the grass with my good old dog, Candy, the black Lab. I looked up at the building clouds and prayed as hard as I could, "God, could you please take care of my ducks so a fox or wild dog doesn't eat them? They can't help being tame ducks instead of wild ducks. Maybe, God, you could find them another home."

That night it rained hard. I sat at the kitchen table working on my wildflower report for school and my brother was trying to do some English. I wanted to go watch television or go out to the barn but I could never do that if my homework wasn't done. I could smell Candy in the washroom and hoped she'd dry off before bedtime. Mama wouldn't let her in if she were wet. But I needed her to keep me company because I was missing Farouk and Ava.

"What are you doing? Talking to yourself?" My brother poked his face up next to mine. "Don't talk to yourself, I can't think."

"Okay, I won't," I said.

Things were quiet for minute.

"Hey, be quiet, you loony bird," he told me.

"I was praying," I said, defiant.

"About those stupid ducks? God's too busy to listen to some kid and her duck story," he said. I kicked him hard.

Mama showed up then and we both got into trouble. I prayed about my ducks that night.

"I'm sorry but I have to do my job as a mother and those ducks are too much for this family," Mama told me when I had finished. "I love you lots. I think it's not so unusual that you're praying that Farouk and Ava have a good home somewhere." Mama put both hands over my hands as I said the Lord's Prayer.

"Good night," she said, going out the door. Candy crawled from under the bed and up in my arms. I rubbed her ears for a long time before I could go to sleep.

Every day was the same. I couldn't forget the ducks, so one day Mama took me to visit them at the park. But they weren't there. Just a bunch of other Mallard ducks that didn't know me. That night my pop told me that I'd best buck up because the ducks were gone and that was that.

Just as the sun came up the next morning I went outside to see day begin. My pony was standing by the pear tree in the pasture. Danny was too sleepy to ride, so I just sat on him. Candy sniffed around, checking smells that she liked.

Suddenly, I heard a sound and looked up. Two black birds flew toward me. One of them was quacking. They circled and landed near the old chicken coop. I think my mouth just fell open. I ran over there. It was Farouk and Ava—I could tell by Farouk's two toes. I was so happy to see them! They seemed happy to see me, too.

When I told Mama, she shook her head in amazement. "You do have a way with animals, Baby Rose, but you sure don't get it from me. They must be different ducks, though."

"God answered my prayers, Mama."

"Baby Rose, He answers EVERY prayer, don't you forget that—just not right when we want an answer or in the way we want Him to answer. I guess they must be your ducks. We'll fit them in somehow with the rest of your menagerie," she said. Then Mama smiled.

Golden Star Lost

GARNET HUNT WHITE

olden Star didn't come for his food on the morning of August 6, 1992. Where could he be? Glenn, my husband, called until his voice became gravelly: "Golden Star! Kitty! Kitty! Golden Star!"

I called and called until I lost my voice. Then I taped the calls and set the recorder on the porch.

Glenn, Whitey, our dog, and I drove around the countryside, looking for Golden Star. We called and called and used the recorder. We asked neighbors if they had seen our beloved cat. No one had. We looked and searched for ten days, but we couldn't find him.

I fought back the tears that trembled on my eyelids. A sinking anguish knotted my stomach. Glenn's face looked bleak with sorrow. He would leave the house, shove his hands in his pockets, hunch his shoulders forward, walk, and look over the fields.

Glenn and I reminisced about Golden Star. We had always taken him for rides in our station wagon since he was a kitten. When he became older, he and Whitey would race to the wagon when they knew we were going somewhere.

Many times, Golden Star would get carsick if we traveled a distance, so I carried plenty of paper towels and wipes in the car. If he

140

got sick, I would lay him next to Whitey, who would begin licking him. Whitey's massaging seemed to help the cat recover.

Golden Star had always hunted in the nearby meadow. If he caught a mole, a mouse, or a rat, he would bring it to the porch, place it outside the French doors, and meow for my attention.

Glenn's birthday was August 20 and I began planning a get-together for him. "No!" Glenn protested. "I don't want to see anyone."

His sharp disapproval told me he was still grieving over Golden Star. Gladly, I stopped all social preparations, as I didn't want to force myself to look happy. I was grieving, too.

Early on the morning of August 20, Glenn's birthday, a loud pitiable cry jolted us awake. We jumped out of bed and turned on the porch light. We could hear wailing just outside the door. What did we see? A thin, malnourished, burr-covered, hollow-sided, grimy, what appeared to be a cat. A bloody paw pressed against the glass; pleading eyes looked at us.

"Golden Star!" Glenn yelled as he jerked open the door and swooped up the matted fur ball. "Golden Star. You've come home for my birthday!"

After patting Golden Star's head, I ran to the kitchen, warmed a bowl of milk, and brought it to him. When Glenn put him down, Golden Star limped to the bowl, dragging a piece of cord tied around his neck.

It seemed as if Golden Star had been a prisoner. Someone must have stolen him from our home and tied him somewhere. But our cat had gnawed through the cord and struck out for home. We never knew how long or how far he had traveled to get to us. We could only thank God for bringing him home.

After Golden Star's tummy was filled with milk, he and Glenn began celebrating the day together. Glenn brushed, bathed, and towel dried the cat until we saw the snow-white and golden-yellow fur. "This is the happiest birthday I've ever had," Glenn said.

Today, as I write this story, who do you think is curled up on my lap? Golden Star. Yes, Golden Star has us under his paw and we love it.

Lonely Lady's Journey

CAROLYN PIPER

 aising chickens may seem an odd hobby, but for one reason or another I love them. In fact, a sand chair is a standard piece of equipment in my coop, for whenever I need time alone to think, recharge, mope or mourn some happening in life, I head out there and just sit quietly watching the flock.

One of the pleasures of spending time with them is that one learns to recognize distinct personalities within what was once a flock of indistinguishable animals. I have, for example, a rooster without a tail feather to his name who struts around as if he were the Sylvester Stallone of the feathered set. A second rooster, who is achingly beautiful, and a full foot-and-a-half high, acts like Pee Wee Herman on the lam from the mob.

And I have Lonely Lady.

Lonely Lady has always been a bit strange. A Rhode Island Red, bred at a hatchery of gene stock that emphasizes laying eggs, no brains and no brooding ability, she was named by the children of the woman who gave her to me because she was a stark individualist in a flock of conformists. Contrary to her gene pool, she broods every spring,

142

refuses to lay eggs until right before she sits down, and is a world-class escape artist of no small intelligence.

There are times during the year when, like it or not, the flock has to be restricted to their pen as coons and foxes, coming out of a long winter with young to feed, start looking for a quick snack. For the most part the flock seems not to notice that they no longer have the run of the yard, but, being the bull-headed individual that she is, Lonely lady most certainly does notice, and takes sharp exception to the situation.

For one thing, she misses the treats she gets when she wanders into the house to request peanut butter on her rice cake. For another, she is prone to taking long daily walks in the woods. So, while I try to keep her in during the dangerous parts of the year, it rarely works. Make the fence higher and she tunnels under, fix the tunnel and she squeezes through somewhere else.

Eventually I gave up all hope of keeping her confined and grew resigned to knowing that each day, no matter what I did, she, and only she, would soon be out of the pen and on her way to visit the kitchen or off to parts unknown.

Then one late fall day she disappeared. Usually home by dusk, just in time to elbow the others out of the way when the nightly treat bucket arrived, this night she failed to appear. Nor did she return in the days that followed. I knew it was inevitable. You can't act like a 300-pound gorilla, well able to cope with anything the world sends your way, if you are a chicken. Sooner or later you're going to end up on the wrong end of the food chain.

Time passed. Massive amounts of snow came in December. Temperatures dropped way below zero in January and February, followed by the promise of spring in the cold brisk air of March.

It was well into the forties one beautiful mid-March day when I decided to go for a walk. Idly running my eyes along the tree line as I approached the woods, I came to a dead stop, for there—shake my head though I might in disbelief—strolling out from among the trees, was a chicken. A very bald chicken— a chicken with no more than a dozen feathers—but a chicken nonetheless. A chicken, moreover, possessing an unmistakably familiar confidence of manner.

Lonely Lady, after five months of coping with Vermont in the winter, with no shelter or food, was home from her walk. I stood there and watched her head for the coop. Her bare bottom looked like a bad imitation of a rubber chicken one finds in a novelty store. Questions raced through my mind: Where on earth had she been all this time? How on earth had she survived? One look at her told me she had not had an easy time of it. Quite frankly, she looked, and looks, dreadful, and there is a bit of a limp in her usual jaunty step.

But, still, there she was. Against all odds. There she was: home from her walk; waiting at the coop door, impatiently glancing over her shoulder to make sure I was following to let her in.

Lonely Lady is recovering fast, but I am still adrift in awe and wonder at her accomplishment. Modern chickens are domestic animals, and Lonely Lady can no more fly to avoid danger than I can. Animal predators, snow, cold, lack of food—she beat them all. It is at times like this that the wonders and mysteries of life seem limitless, and I hold my breath in reverence at the resiliency and beauty of God's loving care that connects us all to one another.

A Home for Life

DRUE ANN HARGIS-RAMIREZ

ven though it was past midnight, I couldn't sleep. I punched the pillow again, knowing I'd be too tired to concentrate for classes in the morning if I didn't fall asleep soon. Just as I started to drift off, a cat started meowing outside my bedroom window. If I didn't know better, I would have sworn it was my cat Snookums meowing outside. Like a mother who can distinguish her baby's cries from another's, I knew my cat's particular meow.

This was impossible, of course, since my parents had given her to a family who lived more than three miles away. We lived in a hilly area with small farms above us in the foothills. Snookums had been given to a family in need of a barn cat.

A few months before, Snookums had experienced her first heat and had gotten pregnant before we could have her neutered. At first I was thrilled, but once she'd given birth to four kittens, her personality seemed to change drastically. Where once she had been affectionate and loving, sleeping on my bed, usually on the pillow curled around my head, or cuddling on my lap, now she refused to be petted, and hissed and scratched.

145

We had managed to find loving homes for three out of four of her kittens, but not for the fourth one, which I had fallen in love with. It looked just like Snookums—dark browns and golds, with long fur. At eight weeks it was so adorable! My dad wouldn't let me keep them both, however, and said I had to make a choice between the two, Snookums or her kitten

I was torn, but the kitten was so adorable, and Snookums just wasn't the same anymore. In the end, we found a new home for Snookums. Even though she had become so unfriendly, I already missed her, and she'd only been gone for two-and-a-half days. After all, she'd been born in my house and her mother was my mother's own cat.

The meowing resumed—almost a howling, really. I couldn't stand it anymore. I had to investigate. I walked over to the sliding glass doors in my bedroom, flipped on the porch light, and pushed aside the curtain to peer outside.

I couldn't believe it. The cat making such a racket was Snookums! Disheveled and dirty, but it was Snookums! Quickly, I slid open the door and scooped her up in my arms. Immediately, she began to purr. Her fur felt cold and her body thin.

With her in my arms, I rushed down the hall and banged on my parents' bedroom door. Bleary-eyed, my dad opened the door. "What's wrong?"

"Look, Dad. It's Snookums. She came back!"

My parents were as astonished as I had been. My mother hurried to get a bowl of water and open a can of Snookums' favorite cat food. She gulped the meat down without chewing. She was obviously starving. She must have been so intent on making her journey home that she hadn't eaten for the last two-plus days. My dad had delivered her to her new home on early Friday evening and now it was Sunday, or, rather, Monday, since it was after midnight.

"Well, that's it. She's earned herself a home for life," declared my dad.

We were able to find a home for the kitten a few days later. Amazingly, once the last kitten was gone, Snookums returned to her old self. Her favorite places again were my lap and my pillow. She began "talking" to me again, and once more loved for me to stroke her fur.

Nine years later, I married and made the difficult decision to leave Snookums with my parents. My mother and I felt that the adjustment to a new home might be difficult, and we were also afraid she might try to find her way home again as she had done so many years before. While my husband and I were on our honeymoon, my mom said that Snookums slept on my bed almost every night, seemingly certain I would be back soon.

When I came back a few weeks later to collect my belongings, she leaped onto my lap. It was hard saying farewell, once I had packed everything. According to my mother, for several days afterwards Snookums forlornly searched my now-empty bedroom. I missed her immensely, and I guess she missed me, too.

Less than a year later, when my parents announced they would be moving out of state, I took Snookums home with me. She adjusted surprisingly quickly. And she found her favorite places again—my lap and my pillow. I guess her home and heart, was wherever I was.

Snookums died, at the age of 19, from kidney failure, purring in my arms until the end. I miss her still and remember her fondly every Christmas as I hang ornaments on the tree, including the one marked "My Favorite Pet," which includes her picture.

My dad said she had great animal instincts to find her way home, especially since she'd been so young, barely more than one year old, and had never left the immediate neighborhood before that incident. I like to think it was love that brought her back to me. Hers and God's.

Here Comes Charlie

PEGGY WILLIAMS

 had awakened to a glorious sunny day and came through the house throwing open curtains to greet the radiant morning. As I threw back the curtain in my utility room, I stopped and took a second look. Across the street, a police car was parked halfway into my neighbor's driveway. A policeman stood talking with Paula, who was obviously quite upset!

Upon closer observation, I saw several neighbors going in different directions. Some were in the yards while others were going down different streets. Several were snapping their fingers and calling, "Here, boy!"—"Here, Charlie!"

Who was Charlie? Curiosity quickly engulfed my mind. I rushed to get dressed and dashed back to glance out the window again. Everything across the street looked normal. Half-disappointed and half-relieved, I decided to get busy and try to forget what I had seen earlier. Paula knew to call if she needed me.

Little did I know that Paula had agreed to "dog sit" that weekend! Not being a "window watcher," I had missed a lot of comings and goings over the past few days. Unknown to me, life had been quite busy across the street.

148

FINDING THE WAY HOME

A week later, I was pleasantly surprised when I unfolded the weekly newspaper to find on the front page a picture of my neighbor, Paula, with a lovely young lady and a frisky-looking dog. My curiosity was peaked and I began reading. It's totally amazing how much apprehension and excitement one dog can create.

If you ever doubted a dog's devotion to its owner, you never met Charlie! He is a Brittany spaniel with short white hair and reddish brown spots. He belongs to Paula's niece, Emily, and her husband. He lives in Ohio, but apparently knows his way around West Tennessee as well.

Charlie and his beloved family had arrived in Tennessee on Friday and dropped by to see Aunt Paula. While visiting, plans were made for Charlie to sleep over with Paula on Saturday night while his family attended an out-of-town wedding. They would pick him up on Sunday and then return to Ohio.

That, however, was not exactly Charlie's desire.

Saturday arrived and so did Charlie. Into the day, Paula became concerned that Charlie might be lonesome and decided to treat him to an "outing" at the city park. Paula didn't leash Charlie so he romped and played happily, yet he never strayed far. Once back in the house, Charlie was quiet. He wouldn't eat or drink, and Paula feared that he was sick. Paula had not recognized his ailment: Charlie missed his family.

When night came and Paula crawled into bed, Charlie placed his big paws upon the covers, thinking he would sleep with her, but Paula told him, "No! Charlie, you must sleep on the floor tonight." As is normal with many beloved pets, Charlie was used to sleeping with his family.

Waking early on Sunday, Paula let Charlie outside without leashing him. Charlie trotted around, sniffing, hiked his leg several times, and then in a half-second took off across the street, through our yard and out of sight. Charlie was gone!

Frantic, Paula combed the neighborhood. No Charlie! She stopped several people to ask if they had seen him, and finally a dog search was begun. The police were called, neighbors and friends went searching for Charlie, but to no avail.

Paula was crushed, not to mention greatly disturbed, that Charlie had run off. She was sure he had gone up to the highway and someone had picked him up.

How could she tell her niece that Charlie had run away? Enough grief had been suffered in their immediate family—the recent loss of a beloved husband, father, brother—and now Charlie was gone.

Guilt ate away at Paula. She was continually assured by her sister-in-law that God had a way of taking care of small creatures and animals, such as dogs. Her niece continued to talk about how faithful a dog Charlie was and how glad he always was to see them when they came home. Paula continued to apologize over and over about Charlie's caper.

Time passed quickly, and still no Charlie to be found. Finally, time ran out. Charlie's beloved family left for Ohio without him, still faithfully believing he would be found. After all, God's word said, "If you have faith as small as a mustard seed, you can move mountains."

Unknown to all, Charlie was on a trek, hunting his family. He was a rare animal that refused to be separated from his family for even a short time. He had journeyed thirty-five miles, crossing two major highways and was within ten miles of his destination when he befriended a Rottweiler.

The owners of the Rottweiler became suspicious when they noticed the blue rabies tag on Charlie's collar. They checked the information on his tag and graciously called Charlie's veterinarian in Ohio. The next morning, the veterinarian called Emily with the news that Charlie had been found. Happiness abounded!

Telephone lines buzzed and plans were made. Emily's grandparents were to pick up Charlie since he was within ten miles of their home. They left immediately.

Oddly, Charlie recognized the grandparents' car when they arrived, and he tried to jump through the car window while he screamed and howled like someone trying to talk.

Emily happily traveled back to Tennessee, and two days later she and Charlie were reunited.

When informed of Charlie's reactions to her grandparents' car, Emily said, "I find that interesting, since he only sees my grandparents twice a year." She was amazed that he had even found his way toward her grandparents' house, since he had only visited the area four times in his life.

When asked about Charlie, Emily replied, "He's pretty calm and he's exhausted, but he was happy to see me."

With a big smile Emily went on to say, "I'm impressed with Charlie. He's getting to be an old dog—he's ten. I didn't think he had that in him, to go so far and to be that much of a 'best friend.'"

As for Paula, she was just thankful that everything had a happy ending. When I asked her about Charlie, she said, "I think Charlie wanted to find Emily. I never heard of anything like that in my life, and if God gives animals the sense to do things like that, we, as human beings, shouldn't worry."

Gone with the Wind-ow

PAMELA SUE COGHLAN

hett Butler will be remembered by movie fans everywhere as a dashing, daring, somewhat reckless adventurer who was tamed, for a short time only, by the wiles of Scarlett O'Hara.

In March of 1985 we adopted our own Rhett Butler, a one-half Abyssinian, one-half traveling salesman—but handsome as Clark Gable. We knew from the beginning that Rhett would be an inside cat and the only adventures he would know would be what could be viewed from the front porch or the upstairs window.

We did a lot of traveling for our business, and our Golden Retriever, named Scarlett O'Hara, of course, would accompany us. I used to miss Rhett terribly when we were away so I encouraged my husband to attempt to travel with him. All my cat friends said cats don't like to go.

We put Rhett in a large dog-training cage where he had room for his regular-size litter box, food, water and toys. He could look out and be a part of the family. On the first few trips he whined, as cats do, unless I took him out of his cage and held him on my lap. Then it became a pattern. If I was in the car I would hold Rhett on my lap where he would purr and look out the window, perfectly contented.

After two-and-a-half years we gave Rhett a little more freedom. When we made stops and left the van, he would jump off my lap and find a comfortable place on the floor of the van.The windows were such that he could not fit his body out of them. We had two that were screened and a roof vent. So he was perfectly safe. When we returned to the car, he would usually come out of his hiding place and go back on my lap.

On a trip to Vermont, Rhett and Scarlett joined us. The heat and humidity were unbearable, so we were careful that when we left the van, it was for a short while. On our way home down Route 7 in the Berkshires of Massachusetts, we made several stops at shops—every time I got back in the car I would pick up Rhett to sit on my lap. The heat was such that he would take naps under the seat, so after a while I didn't attempt to pick him up.

At 5 P.M. we stopped at a gas station and I pulled out the pet food. The sound of the dog's dry food always excited Rhett and he would come out of his hiding place and patiently wait for his dinner. Strange...he didn't come out. I called him. We took all the suitcases and packages out of the car. We looked inside all the packages. No Rhett! INSTANT PANIC AND FEAR! Could it be that he was not in the car? How did he escape? Did he shrink and get through the crack in the window?

Here we are on an island in the middle of a six-lane highway during rush hour in Lenox, Massachusetts. Okay! Be calm! How could I be calm? I was on my way home to have an emergency operation. Due to excessive bouts of hemorrhaging I had become anemic. I just couldn't relax. I started to cry. My husband was more rational. We would backtrack all the way to the last place where we thought I held him on my lap. Memory plays funny tricks: we both had different opinions of where that was.

Before leaving the gas station we searched there and across the street, which was a car dealership. We looked under every car on the lot. We left our card with the car place and also the gas station. Then we departed and started to stop at each place we had stopped at on the way down. Our problem was that the stores were starting to close, so we had to work quickly.

We found out that there are cat lovers and there aren't. We stopped on North Street in Pittsfield, Massachusetts. Several shops there had their doors open, so we asked if they had seen a cat run by. They hadn't, but were sympathetic and took our card.

We checked the alley and the dumpsters. What we weren't remembering was that Rhett was an inside boy and didn't know about the streets, survival, cars and highways. He also had no collar or ID. We would tell people that he was an Abyssinian and they didn't know what that was. His markings were unusual, so he wasn't an easy cat to describe.

We called the police and they were polite, but we could tell what they were thinking: we have too many important things to do than to stop and fill out a lost-cat report.

Then we moved out to the countryside of Lanesboro. This was more frightening since it was woods, cemeteries, highways, many hiding places and fewer people. One man recalled that his dog barked at a strange cat about an hour and a half ago. Could that have been Rhett? We started combing the hills, calling his name. Even if he was there, he would be too scared to come out. We leave our cards with the police and speak to the dog warden. It is a shot in the dark.

As time goes on and it is starting to get dark, the realization is that we will never see our cat again. That is a tough feeling to describe. We had already put one dog to sleep, and even having Scarlett now could not erase the aching emptiness, but this was equally as painful, adding guilt and responsibility. Then we started to pray that maybe Rhett would be found by a kind person and have a nice life in New England. When we saw dead animals on the side of the road, we were brought back to reality.

We decided to go back to Pittsfield. Maybe someone had found him. We walked around the alley and ran into Mike, a nice young man who owned three cats. He said he would keep his eyes open and he helped us look in dumpsters. As we talked, several stray cats wandered by us. Our chances seemed so slim.

My husband went into the print store which, miraculously, was open late. The man said his machines were off for the night. We explained the situation and he printed fifty copies of Lost Cat signs and then didn't charge us. The pet store down the street also said that if our cat was found, they would keep him and feed him until we would get back from New Jersey, which was four hours away. Another kind person. The pet store owner also said to try the ASPCA.

At 9:30 that night we drove there, lucky again that the light was on and the caretaker was up. He said, "I don't want to dim your hopes, but you are looking for a needle in a haystack. Someone will pick up your guy and, if he is cute, feed him and take him in. Then after a month they will get tired of him and bring him over here. They won't say he was found. They will just say that they don't want him anymore. By then any signs or newspaper ads will be forgotten and it will just be another cat." We left our card anyway.

Back to the police station again, this time to fill out a formal report. When the officer saw that we lived in New Jersey, he made the comment, "You mean you would drive all the way back here to get a cat?" How could people be so insensitive?

Now it is 10 o'clock at night. All we had left to do was call a few vets and leave word on the possibility that someone would bring them an injured animal. Then we had to hang the Lost Cat signs on trees from Lanesboro to Lenox.

I kept pinching myself and saying that this was a nightmare and that I would wake up and all the pain and suffering would be over. In addition I was physically suffering from the anemia and the prospect of the surgery I would be having the next day. We also hadn't taken the time to eat. That seemed unimportant.

The long ride home to New Jersey, the feelings of desperation, emptiness, despair...I remember looking at the stars and hoping that Rhett was safe and had found shelter under that big sky.

Arrival in New Jersey was at 3:30 A.M. I turned on the phone machine. Mike, the boy from the alley, said, "I need more info on your cat. I think I know where he is." A glimmer of hope. Then three more calls from a woman named Bernice who said, "I was coming home from bingo and saw a strange cat sitting in the windows of the dry cleaning shop. The cat looked like my grandson's cat from afar. Then I saw the Lost Cat sign on a tree. I still thought it was my grandson's cat. I went to my apartment above the cleaners and mentioned it to him. He went down, looked at the cat and then connected: 'Could it be the cat from New Jersey?'" Another ray of hope.

We called the police and asked if they could send someone to the cleaners. I knew they thought we were nuts. Maybe in the morning they could, but not now.

At 6 A.M. we started. We called the cleaners, for if the owner came in and didn't know there was a cat there, Rhett could run out. Maybe it wasn't even Rhett, but we still were clinging to a shred of hope. no answer...no answer. Why were we so far away and feeling so helpless?

We were brazen and called Bernice, waking her up. She was so kind and said she would wait by the cleaners so that when he opened up the cat wouldn't run out. Sitting by the phone and waiting was torture.

A phone call from Bernice, saying she can't catch the cat or get close enough to identify it. We suggest that she call the ASPCA for help. Another hour goes by. I call the pet store and the owner's wife says she will help with cages, food, etc. Waiting by the phone some more. Then a call from Bernice, saying the ASPCA threw a net over the cat and took him to the shelter.

At this point we are still not sure if this is Rhett. A phone call from the ASPCA saying that the cat was sure nasty—hissing, spitting, grunting—but is it Rhett? We describe all the body markings, the number of stripes on his tail. The guy puts us on hold, comes back and says, "I think so."

I have to be in the hospital in two hours. My husband was planning to go with me. Instead, he gets back in the van with Scarlett, the Golden Retriever, and drives back to Pittsfield, Massachusetts, in hopes that Rhett will be there. I go to the hospital and anxiously wait for word. Time moved so slowly that day. A lot of praying. The phone rings in the hospital and the words are: "We have Rhett." A miracle...another chance...Thank you, God.

The kindness of the people in Pittsfield was overwhelming. The co-incidences of meeting Mike, who lived with Bernice, his grandmother, who just happened to walk by the dry cleaners and happened to see our sign...a miracle. A miracle that the cleaners locked Rhett in for the night and protected him from street dangers and traffic.

Waking up from surgery, I find my husband not there, as promised. Then a phone call from my close friend, telling me Rhett is at the vet. What now? It seems his flight from the van ripped up the pad on one foot, the price one pays for adventure. But the vet says it is not infected. Her only message was to get a collar for the cat.

Waiting to go home from the hospital, my only thought was thinking about holding Rhett. On the way home, my husband kept telling me all he got from Rhett was hissing, grunting, spitting. I justified all that by saying that Rhett had been through a trauma. He was scared.

Walking into the house, seeing Rhett so indifferent he wouldn't let me touch him, reminded me of the infamous line from *Gone With the Wind:* "Frankly, my dear...."

So that is the story of my beloved Abyssinian boy who used up almost all of his nine lives in Pittsfield, Massachusetts. Now all is back to normal, and everyday we thank God for our second chance.

Comfort in the Hard Times

When these things

begin to take place, stand up

and lift up your heads...

(Luke 21:28, NIV).

The Day the Cows Could Count

KATHRYN MAYS
AS TOLD TO LONNIE HULL DUPONT

I grew up on a small dairy farm in northern Michigan. We had about fifty head of cattle at any given time, and it was my chore in the morning to help my father milk them before he left for his work as a high-school teacher. My brothers and sisters joined in the milking again after we came home from school. In my sixteenth year, something happened on the farm that not only convinced me that God was looking out for me, but also that God has a sense of humor.

I loved the farm, and I loved the ritual of milking. I was the oldest of five children, but this early morning chore was something I did alone with my father, whom I have always adored. Each morning the cows would wait patiently outside the barn for the milking. Dad and I would usher them inside, six at a time, milk them, then usher them back out the other side of the barn through a different door. While we hooked them up to the milking equipment, I would think about my day and my life. It was usually dark and often cold—sometimes extremely cold—but the cows' steaming breath and their passive trust always warmed me up. It was a fine way to start a day.

Cows must be milked twice a day, no matter what. If they aren't milked, they can get mastitis, a not uncommon infection, for which they need antibiotics. This renders a cow's milk unusable until she heals up. Even when a cow is sick, however, she has to be milked, and that milk cannot be consumed or sold. It must be poured out.

One time I had neglected to separate the mastitis milk from the rest of the herd's daily take. That evening, my father made me pour the entire day's milking down a drain in the barn floor by myself. None of that day's milk from any of our cows could be sold. I cried the entire time I poured. Dad wasn't unkind; he simply wanted me never again to forget this important—and expensive—detail. And I never did forget.

One Sunday when I was sixteen, my family was away for the day. I don't remember why I was alone, but night milking needed to be done, and I'd have to do it by myself. Five cows had mastitis and were on antibiotics. Each cow had a number attached to her ear, and Dad had given me a list of the five infected cows' numbers. The milk from those cows would need to be poured out. The best way to do all this was to separate the infected cows from the rest of the herd, then milk everybody.

At low light, I headed for the barn. There in a small corral were the fifty cows, all crowded together, all waiting for me to milk them. Now cows aren't like horses. They're big and passive and not exactly high-energy, so they aren't the easiest creatures to lead. Getting five specific cows out of this herd was going to be difficult.

First I'd have to weave in between them and read their numbers to find the right five cows. Then I'd need to throw on a lead rope or prod them somehow to get each one of them out of there and herded into another pen without the other cows getting out, too. And. as I say, cows aren't horses—they don't automatically move aside. They're very curious and, consequently, they may actually get in the way and become obstacles. Or they may just decide to follow an infected cow out of the corral. Then I'd have to get the infected cow into the other pen and the healthy cow back into the corral, keeping the rest of the herd from spilling out. By myself.

So while it wouldn't be an impossible task to separate the five ailing cows from the rest, it wasn't going to be an easy task. Or short. Memories of pouring milk down the drain still smarted. I didn't want to mess this up.

I opened the gate and entered the corral. The cows—as cows are wont to do—turned as a group and stared at me. I looked at the herd. The herd looked at me. I suddenly wished my siblings were there to help.

It occurred to me that God cares about all the details of our lives—of my life. Perhaps this was a time to enlist the Lord's help. So while I held the list of numbers in one hand, I raised my other hand in the air—it seemed appropriate to do that. Then, with all the faith of a child, I spoke in a loud voice toward the heavens: "In the name of the Lord Jesus Christ, would the following cows please step forward? Numbers 2, 11, 17, 32, and 49."

I don't know why I said that or even why I said it that way. I felt pretty silly and was glad no one else was around. But as soon as I finished speaking, I heard a rustling noise from the back of the corral.

You know what happened, of course. Cows numbered 2, 11, 17, 32, and 49 wriggled their way through the herd and came forward. And other cows actually stepped aside for them. I was reminded of the parting of the Red Sea. I picked my jaw up from the ground, opened the gate, herded each of the five into the other pen, then locked the rest of the amazingly cooperative herd back up to prepare to milk. Separating the sick cows probably took me all of two minutes, and milking that early evening took no more time than usual.

I didn't tell my folks about it that night. In fact, I usually never tell this story. Who would believe it? It's the only time something like that has ever happened in my life. But I never forgot it, and I've always appreciated it.

As I said, I like to think God has a sense of humor—we're made in his image, after all. It's true that on that day God smiled on me and made the work of this young laborer a little easier. But when he used a herd of dairy cows as his agents, I like to imagine that he winked, too.

Miracle Dog

CRYSTAL WARD KENT

atie was not a miracle dog in the television sense. She never pulled me from a burning building or fought off an intruder. She didn't wake me in the middle of the night because she sensed I was ill. She did none of those things, yet she saved me nonetheless.

In early 1987, my life was going along on its usual course. I had a job that kept me very busy, a fairly active social life, and since all my family lived close by, I saw them regularly—especially my younger sister, Laurel.

Laurel and I were only two years apart and had always been close. We'd shared a room growing up, and in high school our circles of friends frequently overlapped, so there were many joint outings and parties. We even went to the same college, where again our social circles often intertwined. After college, Laurel and I still lived near each other, so staying in touch was easy. We talked daily, and connected regularly for shopping expeditions, movies or the beach. We both fully expected to marry, settle near each other, and spend many years watching our children grow up together. In fact, we often joked about probably outliving our husbands and sharing an old house with a couple of cats.

Those dreams were abruptly shattered in March of 1987. My sister and I were planning a trip to Florida in early May, the first big trip we had ever taken together. My job was stressful and I needed to get away; she was recovering from a broken relationship, and the idea of a trip to somewhere warm and fun appealed to us both. I still remember her phone call.

"What a trip we've got!" she laughed. "We've got to have new clothes! Let's go to the mall next Saturday." I teased her about her blind date that night, and we agreed to attend a basketball game that weekend. Then a work appointment arrived and I had to go. I didn't know then that it would be the last time I'd hear her voice.

Sometime that day, an insidious bacteria invaded my sister's system. It swam through her bloodstream and began attacking the tissues around her spinal cord and brain, then her major organs. To my sister, it seemed like a bad case of the flu, but it wasn't. It was meningitis, and that night, while my sister hunkered down with blankets and ginger ale, hoping to feel better in the morning, the clock counting the hours of her life was ticking. Bacterial meningitis allows only a 14-hour window for possible successful treatment. That time had just about passed when Laurel went to the hospital the next day.

Initially, the emergency room staff thought Laurel had the flu. The symptoms fit, and there were numerous cases going around. They gave her fluids and something to settle her stomach, and she began to feel better. In fact, my mother called from the hospital, saying they would be home around 11 a.m. I went to do errands.

However, the hospital had done bloodwork as a precaution, and one physician was concerned with what he saw—a high white cell count. Laurel's blood pressure was also low. He ordered a spinal tap, but before it was completed, they knew. Laurel broke out in purple blotches, a tell-tale sign of meningitis. She was whisked to Intensive Care, but within the hour she lapsed into a coma. By nightfall, the doctors were preparing us for the worst.

I had started a prayer chain that afternoon. When I initially visited my sister that evening, I was confident she would recover. She was far too young to die. It couldn't be happening, not to us. But as I stood in her room, clad in the required protective gear, I knew. I knew she was gone. Her heart was still beating, but her brain had long since left.

165

I took her hand, noting how small her hands were, much like a child's. I spoke to her, but felt no connection. My Laurel, my best friend, was dead.

The next weeks and months were a blur. So many family and friends to tell, funeral preparations, her apartment to clean out, notices to send and bills to pay. Our wonderful trip changed. I invited our friends to dinner and distributed mementos. I went back to work. I tried to pull life back to normal, but I couldn't, and I knew it never would be. Then came that horrible first Easter, my dad's birthday, and then mine. It struck me how forever after there would never be anyone who got me the same kind of goofy gifts and cards that Laurel had, how I would never shop for her, or see her seated across from me at family dinners. I remembered the red dress like mine that she loved. I had bought it for her for Christmas, and it became the one she was buried in. I went to call her a thousand times a day to tell her some bit of news. I knew her apartment was rented and she was gone, but I could never bear to cross her number from my address book.

The flood of memories and "nevermores" was overwhelming. I wondered how I would go on. To my friends and family I was strong, but inside I was broken and lost.

By summer, my brother had met a special girl. We all knew Hazel was "the one," and her presence in Lance's life was helping him heal from Laurel's death. I longed for a relationship to heal me. When it came it didn't take the form I expected.

It was a lovely summer evening. I had to go in to work especially early the next day and was getting ready for bed. My brother appeared at the foot of the stairs and called up to me. I was a bit annoyed at the interruption but went to the doorway. Lance stood in the shadowed stairwell, holding something; I wasn't sure what. I only knew he was grinning from ear to ear. I took a step down and saw the brightest puppy face I had ever seen. The dog beamed happiness, and the fat little body wriggled from head to toe as I approached.

"It's a puppy," my brother said, stating the obvious. "It's ours. We're going to call her Katie."

It had been many years since I'd had a puppy. It had even been many years since I'd had a dog. My last dog had died some time before, and with work and school, I had yet to get another. This one was clearly a mixed breed. She was black with a white blaze and chest, and four white paws. The tip of her bushy tail, which was thumping mightily, was white, too. Bushy eyebrows adorned her face, giving her a particularly expressive look.

Lance and I sat right down and watched Katie amble back and forth between us. When she tried to run, she tumbled over after a few steps, rolled around, then bounded up again. We both laughed and laughed.

That summer, Katie was my salvation. I spent hours petting and playing with her. We played toss-the-bucket and fought mightily over sticks and tug toys. She slept in my lap or by my side under a tree. The Fourth of July and other family celebrations passed with less pain because Katie was there with her merry face and playful antics. She breathed love and I drew it into all the empty places of my heart.

As Christmas approached, I felt a pang over not being able to shop for my sister, as I had only the year before. I thought of the one less stocking hung by the stairs. But my pain was eased by Hazel's stocking joining ours, and Katie's. Katie was as excited as any child by the tree and the gifts being wrapped. She loved parties and this felt like a really big one! On Christmas Day, she stood by, quivering with anticipation as one by one we unwrapped our presents. Finally, it was her turn. Patiently she watched as we drew out a ball, a squeak toy, and some treats. Then she went wild, grabbing toys, giving kisses, the tail thumping the entire time. To my surprise, I found myself laughing and having a good holiday. What could have been one of the darkest days of the year had been turned around by an eight-month-old dog!

As the New Year came, and the first anniversary of Laurel's death approached, we all were touched with sadness. But as March passed, and spring bloomed, Katie's antics helped us recover once again. Soon it was her birthday, and no one enjoyed the day more. My mother gave her a large "gourmet" dog biscuit which Katie took almost reverently. She then carried it carefully over behind some shrubs and buried it! My mother was never sure if this meant it was a special gift and had to be saved for later, or if it was incredibly offensive in some way!

As those first hard years passed, Katie was my rock, my companion, my comforter. On days when the tears still fell, she licked them away. On days when I felt lonely, she was there with a tennis ball, plainly saying "Come and play! Let's have some fun!" And we did. On days when the road ahead seemed so very long, she was there, leading me off on a tramp. The walk would clear my mind and boost my spirits as Katie always found plenty to explore along the way.

Katie reminded me that life is good, and that we must always keep on living. She took joy in every simple thing—puddles, snow, piles of leaves, a flock of birds overhead, a good squirrel chase, a new tennis ball. When I looked at life from her perspective, I, too, could find joy each day. As time went by, those moments of joy increased, and I knew I was healing. My life would go on—without Laurel and our plans, yes—but it was still a good life and it was mine to live.

Katie also taught me about time. She always stopped to smell the flowers—and everything else—and she lived each day to its fullest. She sniffed the morning air as if she savored it, as if she'd never smelled anything quite that wondrous before. Some days she had me sniffing, too. Occasionally, I'd catch a whiff of the sea amongst the odors of damp pine spills and meadow grass, and marvel that I'd never noticed it before. The way Katie lived reinforced the message of Laurel's death—never take tomorrow for granted. Take today and embrace all it has to offer, and especially embrace those you love.

From that summer on, I made sure that living was my first priority—not career, not social obligations, not chores, but time for my family, my friends, and the beauty of the world around me.

Wings of Comfort

ANNE CULBREATH WATKINS

huddled miserably in my porch chair, staring out across the rain-drenched fields. A few days earlier, a car accident had taken the life of someone I cared about. As if that wasn't bad enough, it had been raining for more than a week, and my soul felt as dreary and gray as the weeping sky.

From inside the house, the telephone shrilled a summons and I rose to answer it. As I spoke to the caller, I let my gaze wander around the room. To my surprise, I noticed a large black butterfly perched on the screen of one of the open windows.

Hoping not to frighten it away, I tiptoed quietly to the window and studied my visitor. It was a beautiful specimen. There were powder-blue markings on the topsides of the broad, dark wings, and pale orange blotches on the undersides. Curiously, the butterfly uncurled its long proboscis to probe the fingertip I offered. When my phone call ended, I turned all my attention to the lovely creature.

"What are you doing here?" I whispered. The butterfly daintily explored the screen, placing its feet carefully at the edges of the tiny openings. It seemed in no hurry to leave, and indeed appeared to be taking notice of me. After what seemed like a long time, it fluttered its wings and lifted off. The papery rustle of those lovely wings sounded like music to me, and I realized that for a brief time, the ache in my soul had been forgotten. Then it came crashing back, like relentless waves on the ocean shore, and I returned to my chair on the porch.

A hummingbird feeder hung a few feet from where I sat and busy hummers buzzed all around it. The rain hadn't dampened their spirits, and they squabbled noisily around the nectar ports. Normally, I would be laughing in delight at their antics, but now I watched them through a haze of tears. Blurry little birds dipped and whirred, and I wondered if these tears would ever stop.

Abruptly, the phone rang again. I sighed and went to pick it up. It was my husband, and as we spoke, I stepped into the kitchen. Perched on one of the back window screens was another black butterfly! It looked identical to the one I had seen before, right down to the white dots that sprinkled its body, and the ebony legs. The butterfly strolled casually around the screen, then turned its face toward me.

"You're not going to believe this," I told my husband. "But there's been a big black butterfly circling the house and landing on the window screens of the rooms I'm in!"

Allen laughed. "Maybe it's following you."

"Maybe," I said. "Or maybe it's trying to tell me something."

"Could be," Allen agreed. We finished our conversation and I turned my attention back to the lovely winged creature watching me from the window screen.

I rested my forehead against the screen while the butterfly walked about. It seemed comfortable being so close to me, and even occasionally unfurled its delicate proboscis to touch my skin. There was something reassuring about its presence, and I wondered again why it seemed to be following me from room to room. When it finally took flight, the same whispery rustle I had heard before sounded, and strangely, I felt comforted.

Rain pattered against the trees in back of the house, and fell in long straight sheets to soak the front yard. I settled again in my favorite porch chair and watched as colorful butterflies danced around in the droplets. I didn't know that butterflies could fly in the rain, yet these were. Bright yellow wings flashed against the gray that colored the world and I marveled at their determination.

A sudden whir of wings close to my head startled me and I ducked. The never-ending hummingbird battle raged on, regardless of the fact that I was in the midst of their battlefield, and I wondered how they kept from doing each other real harm. Then, to my amazement, the big black butterfly appeared!

It fluttered and floated, angling its way toward the hummingbird feeder. It ignored the fussy little birds that attempted to drive it away, and settled at one of the feeder ports. I could see it flicking its tongue against the port as it sipped the nectar. That was the first time I had noticed a butterfly at the feeder, and certainly the first time I had ever seen one eating there.

Just then, three hummingbirds perched at the other ports and began to sip, too. I was stunned. These tiny birds, who never even wanted to share the feeder with each other, were peacefully enjoying refreshment alongside the black butterfly. What I would have given to have a camera to capture this unbelievable thing that was happening right before my surprised eyes!

All too soon, the meal ended and the hummers took to the air again. The butterfly lifted off, too, and drifted about on the shifting air currents. I held my breath as it slanted toward me, then watched in delight as it deliberately perched next to my arm. In wonder, I reached out a fingertip and carefully touched the butterfly's silky body. It sat still and let me caress it for several seconds before it flitted away.

That black butterfly stayed on the porch with me until it was almost dark. I stared in awe as it danced and dipped and hovered in my space. Several times it landed on porch furniture near me, or on the wall behind my head. I watched the butterfly until it was nearly too dark to see. The last glimpse I had of my visitor was when it perched on the porch rail one last time. It dipped its wings in farewell, then sailed off into the dusk.

It had been an amazing afternoon. One determined black butterfly had accompanied me for hours. A butterfly and three hummingbirds had dined together, and I had witnessed butterflies dancing about in the rain. And while I still had plenty of grief to handle, for chunks of time on that rainy day my attention was diverted and my heartache soothed. My bruised and battered spirits had been lifted by lovely wings of comfort.

The House Blessing

T. J. BANKS

A lot of times, as I found out, you get a half-Abyssinian. Which is not a bad thing, mind you. But sometimes you get the whole Abyssinian.

I had wanted an Abyssinian cat ever since I'd read Gladys Taber's *Amber: A Very Personal Cat*. Granted, we did have Zorro, a charcoal-gray Aby-tabby mix—"We can always sell him as a rare black Abyssinian," my husband Tim used to say—who had wandered into our yard when he was 8 months old and who, after checking our house out, had decided we were worth staying with. And despite his coloring and the conspicuous tabby stripes on his mottled coat, he had the agility, dexterity (he's the only one of our cats who has ever figured out that he needed to put his paw *around* a doorknob to make Things Happen), and highly intuitive way of communicating with people that, as I later learned, marked his purebred relations.

But my Abyssinian dream seemed destined to remain just that. After Tim's death, I went to a Cat Writer's Association (CWA) conference out in California and stopped in at the cat show next door. I found myself lingering by the Aby cages; later, I returned to the room I was sharing with my fellow cat writer Sally Bahner and sheepishly took a handful of Aby breeder cards out of my pocket.

"I think it's a sign for you to get an Abyssinian cat," Sally remarked with amusement.

I chose to ignore the sign then. But the Abys found me anyhow. They're very determined that way. Watch them at a show sometime and notice how they keep trying to jimmy those locks on their cages. Three years later, I hooked up with a couple of Aby breeders, one of whom, Mary Ellen Hape, became a good friend and mentor. From her cattery, Singin', came Damiana, a Blue Aby kitten whom my cattery, Damiana-z, was named for, and Celtic Fire (a.k.a. Celtie), a Red Aby spay. From another out-of-state cattery came an amber-eyed Ruddy kitten whom my daughter Marissa and I saddled with a name that was bigger than she was: Summer Solstice.

From the beginning, Solstice was an odd mixture of shyness and playfulness. She came across as being more self-effacing, less people-oriented than either Damiana or Celtie; but she was also the wise-guy kitten, the one who always started the wrestling matches and play-fights. She was undersized and fighting an upper respiratory infection that just wouldn't quit. She'd go around the house making these snuffling snort-hog noises, which sounded bizarre coming from such a dainty feminine-looking kitten. Despite this, she managed to acquire an ardent beau in Topaz, our young Flamepoint Siamese. He was, and is, nuts about all our Aby girls—their little pointy faces and Dumbo ears apparently make his heart sing—but Solstice with her scrappiness and her whiskers that were too big for her cougar face was the Song of Songs, as far as he was concerned.

We lost beautiful big-eyed Damiana to some unforeseen genetic complications a few months before her first birthday. That left Solstice as the sole hope of our cattery. But she wasn't really putting on weight, and Tom, our veterinarian, had a hunch that those snort-hog noises might be due to a polyp in her throat, similar to one he'd removed from Damiana's. His hunch turned out to be uncannily on target: he removed a sizable polyp and pronounced Solstice ready to go to an upcoming cat show, and then up to Mary's cattery in Rochester, New York, for stud service.

What followed was probably the longest honeymoon in cattery history. Every week for three months, I called Mary for an update on Solstice's romance with a Fawn male, only to learn that there wasn't any.

Truth be told, Solstice sounded as forlorn as any child who'd been sent to summer camp or boarding school against her will: and my heart really did smite me every time Mary told me how pathetically eagerly my little "Cougar-ette" would greet her whenever she came into the room. And long-nosed Topaz ("He looks like Charles deGaulle," my vet said.) wandered around the house, moping for his beloved.

But another, far more serious problem arose. Despite the surgery she'd gone through the previous March, Solstice was having trouble breathing again. A visit to Mary's vet confirmed that the polyp had come back in full force: in view of that fact, there seemed to be no point in putting her through the added stress of breeding. "Spay her," Mary told me over the phone. "Keep her as a pet and just love her."

No problem there. As I was driving up to the Sturbridge cat show a week later to pick Solstice up, I worried, though, that *she* wouldn't remember *us* after her three-month honeymoon-that-wasn't-really-a-honeymoon-at-all. But when I unlatched her carrier door, Solstice bolted straight out of it and up into my arms.

I knew you'd come, those eloquent amber eyes of hers said. *I knew you wouldn't forget me....*

"I never saw a cat so glad to go home," Mary said emphatically.

One hurdle jumped, two to go. First, there was the biopsy to make sure that the polyp wasn't malignant. *No,* I thought, remembering Damiana with her enormous far-seeing eyes and even more enormous ears, *not this one, too.* But the biopsy was negative, and Tom went ahead with surgery, spaying her and removing a seven-ounce polyp. The wonder wasn't that she'd been going about making those ungodly noises but that she'd been able to breathe at all.

She began vacuuming up food. Dry cat food, canned cat food, people food—it didn't matter. Solstice was an Aby with a mission, as far as eating went. *You never know,* the amber eyes would say as she quizzically sniffed a rice cake. By the time her stitches came out, her weight was up to 5.7—a whole pound heftier than she'd been prior to this last operation.

I believe in signs. And Solstice's complete recovery, coming so soon after the loss of Damiana and several other family pets, was proof positive that we'd finally made our way out of that sad, dark grieving place. There *were* happy endings. Bad things *could* be turned around. And good things *did* happen to good kitties.

On my living-room wall is a small gilt-framed piece of poetry entitled "The House Blessing." I never knew who wrote it, but the author certainly knew how to "turn a phrase:"

> *God bless the corners of this house,*
> *And be the lintel blest;*
> *And bless the hearth and bless the board*
> *And bless each place of rest;*
> *And bless each door that opens wide*
> *To stranger as to kin;*
> *And bless each crystal window pane*
> *That lets the starlight in;*
> *And bless the rooftree overhead*
> *And every sturdy wall:*
> *The peace of man, the peace of God,*
> *The peace of love on all.*

One morning—oh, maybe a month or two after the surgery—I happened to turn and see Solstice sitting on top of the radiator right under the poem. Always a pretty little cat, she had just then what I could only call a glow, a positive *aura*, that radiated from her big cougar-eyes straight down to her apricot underbelly.

"Are you 'The House Blessing'?" The words were out of my mouth before I realized it.

The amber eyes deepened appreciatively. *I was wondering when you'd notice,* they said gently.

Sometimes you get the whole Abyssinian. And sometimes, as with my little Soul-Cat, you get a miracle.

176

You Knew All Along

ANN VITALE

ynn slumped down on the couch in the living room. What should have been a joyous visit to the hospital had ended in uncertainty and sadness. Her eldest daughter had given birth to Lynn's first grandchild that morning, but the little boy was jaundiced and had a fever. The doctors had no answers yet for Kenny's unexpected problems.

Thunder, Lynn's big male Newfoundland dog, padded quietly into the shadowed room and sat in front of her. He was sagacious and gentle, as a Newfoundland should be, and edged closer as Lynn sobbed for the young parents and their tiny son. She stroked the dog's soft fur and told him about her fears.

Thunder went to the basket that held his collection of stuffed and squeaky toys and rooted around until he found a softball, carried it over to Lynn and dropped it in her lap. But instead of his usual woof and tail-wagging invitation to play, he sat down again, resting his massive head on the couch, his eyes on her face.

Afternoon darkened to evening, and still the distraught woman sat, sometimes crying, mostly just staring at the floor or talking softly to Thunder. From time to time the Newf would move the softball with his nose, tentatively swish the end of his tail on the floor, and lay his head in her lap.

"Goodness," she said at last, "Jim won't be home for hours, and I've forgotten your dinner, haven't I, big guy? And you didn't remind me."

Lynn went to the kitchen and measured out his food. The black dog proved he was hungry by licking up every crumb.

Lynn stood and watched him, but the light in the kitchen seemed too bright for her mood and she returned to her dark nest. She curled up on the couch and pulled an afghan close around her. Every nerve was on edge as she waited for a phone call with some news—any news. Her whole body felt chilled, as though her heart were shutting down with sadness.

Thunder reappeared, surveyed her for a moment, then picked up the softball and again placed it in her lap, pushing it toward her with his nose. He waved his tail twice and lay down beside the couch.

Lynn spent the night in the living room, telling Jim she wanted to be ready if their daughter called. Thunder stayed, too, instead of opting for his bed in their room.

It was almost dawn when the phone rang. Their daughter had the doctor's reports. The infection causing the fever was already responding well to antibiotics and the jaundice had no particularly dangerous origin. Many babies had it, and a few days under special lights should take care of it. The intravenous lines would be removed then, too, and Kenny could probably come home in four or five days.

Thunder sat up, swooshing his tail like a windshield wiper on the carpet. He picked up the softball and dropped it in Lynn's lap again.

"Yes," she said. "There will be a little boy to play ball with you."

Catfish Promises

ANNE CULBREATH WATKINS

hristmas 1998 looked very bleak for my husband Allen and me. Allen was a full-time touring musician and his work had slowed down for the winter. Without a steady paycheck, we fell behind on our bills, and things added up in a hurry. We knew we'd be all right once the touring season started back, but the mortgage and the other bills couldn't wait that long. Foreclosure loomed over our heads, and I worried myself sick about our finances.

And then, just two days before Christmas, a crippling ice storm struck. Beautiful, deadly, unforgiving ice covered the power lines and tree limbs all through the county. Our rural area was especially hard hit—hundreds of trees snapped under the weight of the ice. They sounded like gunshots going off in the woods behind our house. Later that night I heard the heating unit shut off and knew our electricity had been lost. I shook Allen awake. "Help me cover the fish tanks!" I cried. It wouldn't take long for the fish to die once they started getting cold. And the funny little scavengers, our corydora catfish, had just laid eggs all over the tank walls a few days ago. This would surely kill them.

We tossed blankets and quilts over the three tanks. The water was still warm, but the temperature in the house would begin falling soon.

179

Our two parrots were snug in their cages, blankets keeping drafts away from their small bodies. I knew they'd be all right as long as we kept them covered. But the aquariums....My heart sank when I thought about losing all our lovely fish.

There was an old kerosene heater stored on the porch and Allen lugged it inside. Fortunately we had a container of kerosene stored with it and soon had a warm blaze going. We closed off rooms that didn't need the heat and made sure the door was open to the room in the back of the house where our largest aquarium stood. Tired and worried, we went back to bed. I prayed that we wouldn't get up the next morning to find a lot of dead fish.

To our surprise, the house was warm when we got up. Too warm, in fact! The kerosene heater's thermostat switch didn't work and there was no way to adjust the heat. It must have been eighty degrees in the house.

We quickly checked the thermometers in all the aquariums. The temperatures were holding steady, pretty close to what they'd been when the power went off. And all the fish were doing fine, swimming around in their darkened tanks, acting no differently than usual.

Over the next few days we discovered that lots of foods could be prepared over a kerosene heater—beans, eggs and sausages, soup, coffee, even biscuits. At night, when there was no television to watch or stereo to listen to, we got out Allen's guitar and sang our favorite songs. Sometimes we squinted in the semi-darkness over the Scrabble board, or sat closer to the lamps and strained our eyes trying to read. The house was toasty warm and the birds seemed to be enjoying the adventure. Still, my heart sank lower with each passing moment. What were we going to do about all those bills? Somehow, sitting in the near darkness made everything seem worse.

Christmas day arrived, cold, icy, and still with no electricity. We trudged next door to my brother's house, where he had rigged up an electric light bulb to a car battery. We had a wonderful time, opening gifts in the soft light and enjoying a fantastic hot meal cooked on their gas stove. Then Allen and I walked back home, slipping and sliding on the ice-covered road, breathing in great gasps of frigid air. Brilliant stars glowed in the darkness overhead and I tried to imagine how the night skies must have looked to the shepherds all those years ago. Was it as cold and blustery then as it was now?

It was a relief to hustle into our warm house, and I hurriedly checked the aquariums with a flashlight. Everybody was still swimming around, and the temperature in the tanks was a few degrees higher than normal. That old kerosene heater was doing its job well. As I dropped food into the tanks, I caught myself breathing a prayer. "Dear God, if we have dead fish when the electricity comes back on, then I'll know we're going to lose the house. If all the fish are okay, then we'll be okay, too." I knew it was silly, but I found myself clinging to those words over the next few days.

New Year's Eve was rapidly approaching and the power was still off. Some of the roads were passable now and we went out to survey the damage. Our area looked like a war zone. Trees were snapped off, power poles broken, homes damaged, cars crushed under fallen trees. The devastation was widespread and nobody seemed to have any idea when our electricity would be restored.

I checked on the fish often. It was hard to count them in the dark, but I was afraid to take the blankets off the tanks. I'd rather strain my eyes trying to see than to risk chilling them. From what I could tell, we hadn't lost anybody yet. So far, so good.

Then came the day we'd been praying for. There was a hum, a few odd crackling noises, and the lights snapped on. Life was soon back to normal. Allen even got a call to work with a friend of his who needed some carpentry work done, and while this would certainly help our finances, I was afraid it would be too little, too late. With a heavy heart, I went to watch the fish.

There was movement in a big bushy plant in the corner of one of the tanks. "What is that?" I muttered. I stooped down so I could peer more closely into the tank. A teensy baby catfish was busily cleaning the plant leaves!

The prayer I'd caught myself whispering over and over since Christmas night exploded in my mind. "If the fish die, we'll lose the house. If the fish are all okay, then we'll be okay, too."

Suddenly, my heart sang with joy. Not only had all the fish survived, but we had brand-new baby catfish! I knew that everything was going to be all right, thanks to Christmas prayers and promises—and a few little catfish.

That's What Friends Are For

NANCY B. GIBBS

"Daisey's getting to be an old lady," the veterinarian told me, with tears in her eyes. For the third time that year I had taken my little white toy poodle to see Dr. Jennifer because she was having stomach problems. I knew exactly what the doctor was trying to tell me. In human years, Daisey was seventy-seven years old. She slept most of the time and played very little. But the glow in her eyes remained bright when she looked at me.

When we returned home that day, I held Daisey close to my heart. We cuddled the way we did the day she came to live with us. A few tears fell down my face as I thought about the incredible love Daisey had shared with me over the years. I remembered how much she helped me when I was recuperating from emergency surgery and she was just a puppy. During that time, our relationship bonded. I was confined to the house and she didn't leave my side. She became my best friend.

When my children moved away from home to become independent young adults, Daisey took on the role of my child. Many times, on lonesome nights, we sat on the balcony together and talked about the

moon and stars. I told her how God is the creator of a beautiful universe. During the day, we sometimes sat on the front porch swing, watching the birds flying around and the neighbors as they walked by. When we sat outside during the winter months, I wrapped Daisy in her own comforter so she wouldn't get chilled. We both loved every second of our time together in that swing.

One autumn day I was given the news that my father was terminally ill. The doctor's prognosis wasn't good. I panicked every time the telephone rang. I dreaded the day that I would be forced to say goodbye to my father. Those dreadful months were extended to four years, and I don't know what I would have done without Daisey to meet me at the door when I came home in tears. When I cried, Daisey cuddled closer to me. She seemed to understand my grief.

Many people thought I should have been able to accept the plight before me, dry away the tears and get on with life. On the outside I did just that, but everyday when I returned home Daisey allowed me to express my grief and helped me to heal. Her bright eyes gave me courage and hope. I had somebody to talk to, somebody who would not be judgmental. She just allowed me to express my emotions. I'm convinced that those conversations helped me to cope after my father passed away.

When Daisy came into my life I had no idea what a difference she would make. Dr. Jennifer may be right, and Daisy may not have many years left, but until God calls her to heaven, we'll be the best companions we can possibly be. The thought of losing her breaks my heart, but the love we shared together over the years will forever remain a precious memory.

For today, however, I'll cuddle and hold Daisey. We'll rock, talk and sing. She'll give me big, fat, sloppy kisses, just as always. And I'll cherish every moment we have together, even if she is getting older. This "old lady" has faithfully helped me, and I will always be there for her. Simply spoken, that's exactly what best friends are for.

A Prince of a Dog

PHYLLIS HOBE

It was not a good time for me. My mother had died after a long battle with cancer. The company I had worked for was sold, and the new owners down-sized all of us. Then my marriage came apart and my husband and I made plans to sell our house and separate. Only one thing in my life was still there for me: my dog Trooper. He kept me going.

Trooper was a thirteen-year-old Welsh Terrier and I had had him since he was a pup. Originally I planned to enter him in dog shows because he was such a beautiful example of his breed, but he grew a little too tall and no longer fit the breed standards. No matter. I loved him dearly and he was devoted to me. He celebrated my joys and banished my sadnesses.

Like most terriers, Trooper was feisty and feared nothing. Although he got along well with other animals, he always let them know that he was in charge. I remember the time I took him to visit a friend who had a large German Shepherd. As we pulled into the driveway, we saw Scout, the Shepherd, standing in the yard, watching us. He didn't move as I parked the car and got out. Then I let Trooper out and he immediately took off toward Scout. Suddenly I realized what he was going to do. It didn't matter that Scout was three times Trooper's size; Trooper was going to knock him down. I had seen him do it before.

As he approached Scout at full speed, Trooper rolled himself into a moving ball, intending to hit Scout's legs and knock him over. But this time it didn't work. As the rolling furry missile came close, Scout simply stepped aside and let Trooper roll past. Fortunately, Scout was a good-natured animal and seemed willing to overlook the whole incident. But I have never seen a dog as embarrassed as Trooper was. When he came to a stop, he stood up, shook himself and ambled over to some shrubs as if Scout wasn't even there. Several minutes later, he came up to Scout in a friendly manner, as if he had just noticed him.

For most dogs, going to the veterinarian is an ordeal. Trooper took it in stride. In the waiting room, he climbed up on a chair next to me and took a nap while most of the other dogs were panting heavily. He obviously felt comfortable with Dr. Gulliford, our vet, and lounged on the examining table while he got his shots. Just as obviously, Dr. Gulliford enjoyed the visit. "Trooper," he used to say, somewhat paraphrasing William Shakespeare when the examination and shots were finished, "you're a prince of a dog."

From the very beginning, Trooper approved of John, the man I eventually married. And the feeling was mutual, so that when I told John I would like to have Trooper present at our wedding, John agreed. In fact, John insisted we take Trooper along on our honeymoon, and the three of us had a wonderful time. After that, Trooper went everywhere with us, and if he wasn't accepted, we didn't go.

Now that John and I were going our separate ways, I knew he and Trooper would miss each other. I even considered giving him to John, but I just couldn't part with him. I needed him so much.

It was a hectic time. I was following up job leads and going on interviews and looking for a new place to live. And each time I came home I would hug Trooper with all my might and bury my face in his wiry fur. He stayed very close to me, and if I sat down he would climb up next to me, snuggle down, and rest his head in my lap. If I stayed long enough, he would fall asleep and snore so loudly I couldn't help but laugh.

Then I began to notice that something wasn't right. Trooper had never been ill, but all of a sudden he stopped eating. He was listless.

I thought perhaps he was missing John, but something told me it was much more than that. His powerful little body seemed to shrink, and by the second day he could barely stand. I took him to the vet immediately.

Dr. Gulliford was waiting for us when we arrived. He came out to the car, lifted Trooper from the passenger seat and, without a word, took him inside. As I followed along behind them, I reached out to God and prayed. "Lord," I said, "I can't give him up now. He's all I have. Please let me have him a little longer—until I get my life together. But I don't want him to suffer!"

Tests showed that Trooper was very, very ill with a liver malfunction. He was going down fast, and Dr. Gulliford was doing everything he could to save him—intravenous fluids and medications of all kinds. Dr. Gulliford even arranged to spend the night at the clinic. "But you go home," he told me. "You can't do anything here. We'll know in the morning whether he's going to make it. I'll call you."

I don't know how I got home that night because I was crying so hard I could hardly see the road ahead of me. And it was useless to try to sleep without my wonderful furry friend alongside me. I just kept praying.

The phone rang just before dawn. "He's going to live," Dr. Gulliford said.

"Oh, thank you!" I said, bursting into tears.

"No, don't thank me," Dr. Gulliford said. "I can't take credit for this. I've seen this illness before and I've never known a dog to live through it. But Trooper did. There's something—or someone—else at work here."

"I know," I said. "God answered my prayer."

When I went to bring Trooper home, Dr. Gulliford explained that he would need a special diet because his liver would never be normal and would not be able to process some substances. "For instance," he said, "let's hope he never requires surgery because his liver will never be able to handle the anaesthesia."

Trooper looked so much better already, and on the way home he enjoyed looking out the window. "Thank you, God," I prayed. "I'll take good care of him."

Over the next two years I gradually rebuilt my life. Trooper and I moved into a charming little house on an old estate where we had plenty of room for our long walks. I found a job on a newspaper and loved it. I made new friends, and we cared about each other. Through it all, Trooper's love strengthened me. As always, he was there for me.

When Trooper was fifteen, he began having problems. First he lost his hearing, but I had trained him with hand signals as a puppy, so I could still communicate with him. Then he lost his sight, and I knew that his time was up. Since he couldn't see or hear, he felt threatened by everything except me. I knew I couldn't be selfish. I had to let him go.

When I called Dr. Gulliford, all I could say was "It's time." He understood and said he would wait at the clinic for us.

I had one more thing to do before we left our house. "Thank you, dear Lord," I prayed, "for letting me have him a little longer." And in my heart I knew I would have him forever.

Vera and the Mockingbirds

RENIE SZILAK BURGHARDT

 first met Vera in 1983, when I moved to my little farm with the somewhat dilapidated farmhouse. Her forty acres adjoined my twenty-five acres, so she was my neighbor. Already in her upper seventies and a widow of ten years, Vera was one of those memorable women who live out their lives on their beloved homesteads.

"My Dwight passed on ten years ago," she told me on her first visit, when she came to greet me with a freshly baked peach pie, and a welcoming smile. "And my two girls moved on to live their lives in cities, so I guess our farm will be sold to strangers, after I'm gone."

"Oh, that's sad," I said.

"Yes, it is that. Our farm has been in the family since the 1800's. It was Dwight's home place. We lived here since we were married, and raised our family on it, and I'm a-staying here until they carry me away and lay me down to rest next to Dwight, in the little cemetery just a half-a-mile from here. Besides, if I moved, I'd miss my mockingbirds, and they'd miss me." I smiled at her remark, and as she got up to leave, I thanked her for the pie and the visit.

"Now you be sure to come by and visit with me, too," she said. "I love company. When I'm not at church, I'm usually at home, piecing quilts, or making dolls, and I'd love for you to see some of my work."

So the tall, thin elderly lady with the soft, brown eyes, white hair, and warm smile became my friend. Soon, I was over at her place regularly, watching her piece one of her beautiful quilts, or work on her adorable soft, country dolls, or just listening to her stories about life on the farm.

One late spring day, as we sat on her little porch chatting, a mockingbird flew out of a holly bush by the house. It landed on a nearby fence post and began singing its little heart out.

"I guess that's one of your mockingbirds," I said, as the bird finally stopped singing and flew close to the ground in pursuit of an insect.

"Yes, that's one of them," Vera nodded. "They have a nest in the holly bush. They've been using it for several years now."

"How nice. And you think it's the same mockingbirds that nest there every year?"

"Yes, I do believe it's the same pair," she said. "See that platform feeder there, on one of the fence posts? Dwight put that up, years ago. That's where I place my treats for my mockingbirds. They especially love bits of fruit."

"You know, I always thought mockingbirds mainly imitate other birds. But they actually have their own song, don't they?"

"Oh, yes! And a beautiful song it is," Vera said emphatically. "But they are very good mimics. One year, my Dwight actually taught a mockingbird to sing his favorite hymn, 'How Great Thou Art.'"

"You're making that up." I smiled as I said that.

"No, it's true. Dwight was a wonderful whistler. When he whistled, people stopped to listen. One day, after listening to a mockingbird's repertoire, he began to whistle that beautiful hymn as he worked around the yard. And he whistled it, and whistled it some more. A little later, I was sitting on this very porch, sewing one of my dolls, when I heard an unmistakable and beautiful rendition of "How Great Thou Art" ringing from the boughs of my oak tree. A mockingbird had learned it from listening to Dwight whistling it." Tears welled in Vera's eyes as she recalled that special moment.

"Of course, one is not supposed to whistle hymns. But Dwight's whistling was so beautiful that I don't think the Lord could have taken offense at it," she added.

A few years later, I sold that little farm and moved 20 miles away to my present location. However, I kept in touch with Vera, and still went to visit her regularly. One day, about five years later, she told me that she had been feeling pretty "tough" lately, and a checkup showed a spot on her liver.

"The doctor says they could operate on it, but more than likely it wouldn't give me much more time if they did. So I decided against it," she said. "As much as I hate the thought of leaving my mockingbirds, if the Lord is ready to take me, I'm ready to join Him and Dwight."

A couple of months later, one of Vera's daughters came and took her to Wichita with her, where she passed away shortly after, at age eighty-seven. Of course, they brought her back, and she was laid to rest, next to Dwight, in the little country cemetery, shaded by large oak trees.

Recently, I drove back to my old neighborhood to visit a friend who had moved into the area. As I drove on Highway Z and passed Vera's old place, a sense of sadness and nostalgia enveloped me. Her little cottage was boarded up, her field was overgrown, the place looked unkempt. Someone from out of town owned the farm now; someone who didn't care how it looked. Suddenly I felt the urge to visit Vera one more time.

I turned unto the narrow dirt road leading to the little cemetery, just half-a-mile from Vera's home. I parked and walked to the largest of the large oaks, where Vera's and Dwight's grave was. As I stood there in silent contemplation, suddenly a beautiful song filled the silence around me. And, sure enough, it was a mockingbird, singing his heart out from that oak tree above the grave. I was awe-struck!

Coincidence? Perhaps. But I walked away from there with goose bumps on my arms.

Unexpected
Guests

Are they not all ministering spirits,

sent forth to serve...?

(Hebrews 1:14, RSV).

His Reason for Visiting

RUBY BAYAN

y friend and I sat on the floor, leafing through a dusty stack of family albums. Mark wanted me to help him pick out a few interesting photos to scan and post on his new website. We went over the albums as if we were viewing stills of a home movie as each of his three kids came into the world and grew to be the young adults they are now. The snapshots of birthdays, graduations, travels, and holiday festivities immortalized the memories of faces, places, and occasions that Mark's family had encountered through the years.

The photos showed that the kids had been fond of dogs. Various breeds and sizes of dogs showed up in many pages of the albums. But what struck me, as I scrutinized the photos one by one, was a black-and-white long-haired cat that obviously became an important member of the family. He sat with the children on what must have been a memorable Halloween because he was dressed in a colorful clown costume and you could almost detect a smile between his whiskers.

"You had cats?" I asked casually.

"A cat. We had one cat. Harry."

Harry appeared in a couple of Christmas family photos, posing as elegantly as the rest of the family. He frolicked for the kids in several snapshots of them having fun in the backyard. He sneaked in just in time to join a group picture of the family opening presents beside the Christmas tree. And in one of the kids' albums, Harry actually had a dedicated section—a pictorial.

"Harry must've been special to Michelle. She has a pictorial of him here," I said. I became curious because I grew up with cats and I know the kind of impact they can have on people.

"Oh, yes, Michelle was particularly fond of Harry. Well, all of us were. Let's take a break and I'll tell you how Harry came into our lives." Mark helped me off the floor and led me to the kitchen.

While waiting for the coffee to brew, Mark shared a remarkable story.

Their family had just relocated from across the country and the transition was extremely tough, especially for the kids. Adjusting to new schools, starting new friendships, and coping with each other's anxieties stressed everyone to the breaking point. Mark and his wife bickered over their new jobs and responsibilities, and the kids resented having to witness the growing animosity. They were all getting on each other's nerves. The family was falling apart.

Mark remembered that one Christmas Eve, when they were hardly on speaking terms, he had to coerce everyone to dress up and attend mass—to be together as a family, even for one day of the year.

After the mass, as they all quietly hopped into the van to drive home, a curious thing happened—a black-and-white stray cat hopped in, too. They tried to shoo him away and coax him out of the van, but the cat had found himself a nice corner behind the back seats. Mark looked around to see if someone would come looking for a missing cat, but all the churchgoers were busy greeting one another and rushing home to celebrate Christmas Eve.

"Let's go, Dad! Let's just keep him. He wants to come home with us!" It seemed like a long while since Mark had heard his three kids agree on something. He wasn't about to disappoint them, so he drove home. Excited, the children focused on their new friend. The cat's well-groomed longish fur inspired them to name him "Hairy," which later became "Harry."

Harry stayed with the family through the holiday season. For a stray, he looked relaxed, so at-home, and unmistakably an instant member of the family. He had a friendly and loving way with everyone, and everyone loved him back.

"We don't know who really owns him, or where his real home is, so if he suddenly disappears, don't be heartbroken, okay?" Mark warned his kids.

The kids took turns feeding Harry, cleaning out the litter, and brushing his fur. They enjoyed sharing the responsibilities of taking care of their precious pet. Sometimes they'd toss a coin to see who would keep Harry in his or her room for the night. And because the kids got along better, Mark and his wife relaxed and sorted out their differences. Harry had actually brought the family together again.

"That's the story about Harry," Mark concluded, as we walked back to the pile of albums.

"Wait! That's it?" I wanted to know more. "So, how long did you have Harry?"

Mark smiled, "Ah, that's the mystery there. We found him—or should I say he found us—at the church on Christmas Eve. Three years later, also around Christmas time, he disappeared—just as mysteriously as he appeared in our lives. I guess when he had accomplished his mission with our family, he had to move on to help another."

"Is this for real?" I said. I wasn't sure I wanted to believe him. Mark sat down on the floor among the photo albums and smiled.

"Oh, yes, it's for real," he stressed, pointing at more pictures of Harry taking an active part in a lot of activities they enjoyed as a family.

"We will always be thankful for Harry's short visit. He came into our lives to bring our family back together. He's out there now, somewhere, bringing kids and parents back together. It may sound incredible, but, yes, it's for real."

Caliban

HENRY S. F. COOPER

ne day in June, Rachel, a sixteen-year-old, was walking on the hot paths of Central Park, New York City, on her way to my office. Her attention was suddenly caught by a small black object struggling in the grass at the base of a tree. A she came closer she saw that it was a young bird, a fledgling covered with down and pinfeathers. Its wings were spread, and it gasped for breath as it weakly tried to move forward by clumsy efforts of its wings and legs. The small creature was nearly dead of heat and exhaustion. Nearby lay the only refuge it had known—a battered and torn nest which harbored the dead body of one of its nest mates.

The girl's heart was touched with pity. She carried the bird to my office in her cupped hands. Thus Caliban, the grackle, came into our lives. We called him Caliban, because he was such a homely little fellow and he was black as ink.

When Rachel brought the bird to me he was near death. In fact, I was sure that he was going to die. He lacked the strength to raise his head and he could not open his mouth. We gently opened his beak, then took some soft, moistened bread and pushed it down his throat with "thumb" forceps. We made a nest of cotton for him in a box, and when Rachel left my office with the bird I thought he had perhaps two hours to live.

Eleven days later, Rachel called me on the telephone. Caliban was alive all right. She had fed him a mixture of hard-boiled egg, biscuit, raw fruit, and cod-liver oil, and he had grown so big and his wants had become so numerous that he been assigned the only bathroom in the apartment. Worst of all, her mother said she had to get rid of him. Rachel did not feel it safe to let Caliban go free in Central Park because he was still unable to feed himself, although he could fly after a fashion. Could I do anything to help? Fortunately I was leaving for my vacation the next day. I took him to Cooperstown, New York, with me.

The first morning I let Caliban loose in our garden. He immediately flew, and I suddenly realized that his flight control was not yet very good. He could only fly up and not at all down. He headed straight for the sky. It was only by the greatest piece of luck that he managed to catch onto the very top of the tallest tree in the neighborhood, and there he sat. Unfortunately, I had just fed him—so I had to wait about an hour to get him to come down. Then hunger got the better of him and he began to answer my calls. This time he did not trust his wings, but climbed down the tree by hopping from limb to limb.

He immediately worked his way into our hearts. He utterly and completely trusted us. When he wanted food he didn't think or hope he was going to get it—he knew he was going to get it, and he got mad if he didn't. He was completely lacking in the fear that wild creatures seem instinctively to have of human beings. He would nestle in the angle of my elbow; and at first he seemed to like being stroked. Later he disliked being touched, although he otherwise remained fearless of us.

At first we let Caliban go free when we were about, but we put him in an old canary cage at night or when we were not at home. Gradually Caliban developed a great dislike for his cage. Whenever he was locked up he made the house ring with his complaints. On one occasion, however, when he became terrified at being caught outside during a thunderstorm, he flew to his cage like a frightened child and tried every way to get in it.

Gradually we let Caliban free for the whole day, only shutting him indoors in his cage at night where he would be safe from marauders. Soon he realized that sunset meant imprisonment. One evening, when

I tried to catch him, he perched on our chimney top and nothing would tempt him to come down. From that time on we left him out both day and night, and we never discovered where he spent his nights. All we knew was that he disappeared at dusk and reappeared at dawn. In the early morning after his first night out he came to the kitchen door for a handout from our cook. He brought with him ten or twelve other birds that remained in the background and watched curiously while he was being fed. Afterward he flew away with them but soon returned alone. This was the only time that we saw him with other birds.

We came to believe that Caliban thought of himself as a human being. After all, human beings had attended to all his wants from his earliest memory. In fact, we thought it would have been illogical for him to think of himself in any other way. If he was in a tree or hedge he always let us know where he was by his peculiar croaking call. If he saw us from a distance he was very apt to fly to us and alight on the head of one of us, or on one of our shoulders. He especially enjoyed climbing all over us, pulling at our ears, the buttons of our clothing, or at shiny bits of jewelry that we wore. He was particularly fond of anything that glittered or was bright-colored, and he loved to tear matchboxes apart and scatter their contents on the ground. He pilfered cigarettes and cigars, and iced-tea time has a special attraction for him. The tall glasses, the shiny spoons and the ice, the sprigs of mint and the slices of lemon—all these proved utterly irresistible to him. After he had become tired of playing with these he would perch on the edge of a glass and try to take a bath in its contents, refusing to move even when the owner raised it to his lips. If the liquid did not suit Caliban's taste for either drinking or bathing, he would preen his feathers with it. Sometimes he used after-dinner coffee for this purpose.

He was very good at walking and would follow us around by the hour, particularly if we worked in the garden. Whenever we pulled up a weed he would rush in to grab any worm or insect that might have been exposed. He would often start to follow us on foot—and if the pace got too fast for him he would fly to one of our shoulders to ride. If he seemed to want company and saw us inside the house, he would fly to the window sill and tap on the glass with his beak. In the late afternoon, when he often got tired, he was quite apt to alight on my shoulder, snuggle up to my neck, and go to sleep. Just before going to sleep he would usually talk in a low voice, as if to tell me of the events of the day.

For about five weeks Caliban was our constant companion. It would be difficult to evaluate accurately the amount of pleasure he gave us. There was a sad side to it, too—it was obvious that he was adapted to human society but not to bird society. He lived a lonely life in this sense, always on the fringe of humanity—never completely with us, but never with his own kind. He also seemed rather indiscriminate in his fondness for human beings. During this period he seemed to favor me over other people, possibly because I had the most to do with his care. Later on, however, he showed me no more attention than he showed to anyone else.

After my vacation had ended, I returned to New York. Caliban remained at our home in Cooperstown, but the next day he disappeared. We were fearful that he had become prey to a cat, but five days later, when we had given him up for lost, a friend of ours told us:

"My next door neighbor was working in his garden this afternoon when a blackbird alighted on his head and—would you believe it?—he couldn't get rid of him?"

201

We knew Caliban was still living. He had gone to dwell by the riverbank about a quarter mile away. After that he began to range more widely. He seemed to want to be with people, and the more people the better. One little girl said that Caliban awakened her every morning where she slept on a porch. When he arrived he alighted on her head and pulled her ears. A man said that Caliban spent a week with him, helping him in the garden and riding on his shoulder while he mowed the grass. Other people said that Caliban had joined them at a picnic about a mile up the lake—that he seemed to have a good time and that he certainly gave them one.

At the lake front in the middle of Cooperstown is a park frequented by many people in the summertime. There is a stand there where one can buy hot dogs and soft drinks, or rent boats. Caliban moved there about the middle of August, stayed three weeks, and became famous. The owner of the stand wrote:

"My only regret is that I didn't have the camera handy when your bird was performing some of his cutest or boldest or sauciest acts— stealing a cigar out of the box and flying off with it to the park, pecking at ladies' nylons from under a park bench, preening himself in the soapsuds, tossing piece after piece of wrapped gum behind the freezer, attempting to tweek a rose off a lady's hat."

After Labor Day people no longer came to the waterfront park, and Caliban moved to the business section of town. Here he went freely in and out of stores and stayed in one of them four days. He even went into the famous Cooperstown Baseball Museum.

Toward the end of September, Caliban disappeared. Perhaps he went south for the winter. If, on the other hand, tragedy overtook him as the result of his excessive trust in human nature—still his brief life was all to the good. For what bird ever became so famous? He was the talk of Cooperstown, the subject of several newspaper articles, and even the subject of a paper I presented before a learned group of scholars.

Caliban! We named you better than we knew. Seemingly part human—part wild—wholly neither—but living on the borderline between humanity and nature, it was only through the frailest thread of circumstances that you lived at all.

from THE AUDUBON BOOK OF TRUE NATURE STORIES

Remembering Henry

CLYDE GEHMAN

In the the early seventies, my family and I spent quite a lot of time with my parents in the Endless Mountains of Pennsylvania. On the mountain where my parents had their cabin—actually it was an old farmhouse—there was also an elderly gentleman named Dave. Although he lived on the mountain, he had another small cabin about a quarter mile away.

Dave came back up the mountain every day in his old pickup truck. You could hear him coming from quite a distance as the truck banged its way along the dirt road. In the bed of his truck was a basket of apples which he brought for the deer. When Dave parked his truck by his cabin, he would simply get out, look around and yell, "Come get your apples!" It was like magic, the way the deer would suddenly appear. Some people used to say the deer heard him call, but I think they started heading for his cabin as soon as they heard his truck banging up the road.

In this group of deer was a yearling buck that was a lot more curious than the other deer. As spring turned to summer, the youngster got a little braver until he was finally eating apples out of Dave's hand.

Like all animals in this kind of a situation, the buck got a name. We called him Henry, and if Henry was in the area when we called him, he could come running. I couldn't get him to eat out of my hand, the way Dave did, but he would come to within a couple of feet of me and eat the apples.

As the summer wore on and the hunting season approached, I thought maybe this would be my year. I'd been deer hunting for 20-some years, and never saw a legal buck to shoot.

On the first day of buck season, I was standing by a big oak tree on the back of our property. I had seen plenty of deer, but, as usual, no buck. Then, out of the corner of my eye, I caught a movement. Sure enough, this could be my first buck—and it was walking right toward me! Then, all of a sudden, it dawned on me who is was. It was Henry. He walked to within 10 yards of me and stopped and looked at me.

I really didn't need this, and Henry wasn't going to be my first buck. I put my rifle up against a tree and told Henry to get out of there. He just stood there and looked at me. Finally I started waving my arms at him, and he turned around and trotted off.

That night before dinner, my dad asked me if I had seen anything that day. I said yes, that I had one spike deer walk right up to me. Dad asked me if I missed it. I said, "No, I didn't shoot." When he asked me why I didn't shoot, I told him, "It was Henry."

"Oh," was all he said. Then, after a while, he said, "You probably should have taken him, because the next person he walks up to probably will."

"Maybe," I said. "But better him than me."

After dinner in camp, the young guys did the clean-up. My job that night was garbage detail. On my way back to the house after dumping the garbage, I was passing our old barn and I thought I heard a noise. I went to investigate, and as I approached the barn I shined my flashlight around. When I aimed the light into one of the stalls, there stood Henry. As I turned around and left, I know I had a big smile on my face.

Back at the house, I told my dad that Henry had made it through the day. He asked me how I knew that and I said, "I just saw him standing in one of the barn stalls." Dad just shook his head and smiled.

Nobody ever knew how long Henry spent in the barn because after that night none of us ever saw him again. But, after close to 30 years, when friends get together and talk about Dave and Henry, we still get big smiles on our faces

The Gift That Keeps On Giving

GINA ROMSDAHL

I first noticed her in late summer, chasing after butterflies in my garden. My flowers attracted hummingbirds, squirrels cavorted among the trees, and numerous birds flocked to my feeders. The bustling wildlife was inviting to several of the local cats, and I assumed that this white feline belonged to a neighbor. I'd see her now and again, but every time I tried to approach her she would run away.

I returned from a week of vacation in late October to find that winter had arrived in my absence. Snow covered the ground and icicles dangled from the roof. I was surprised to find the petite cat still hanging around my yard, unlike the other neighbor cats who were probably sitting cozily by the fire in their own homes. In fact, her visits were more frequent and my suspicions became aroused when I witnessed her eating suet that had fallen to the ground. She must be awfully hungry, I thought, to be scrounging for food among the birds' leftovers.

I placed some cat kibble near the fence. It disappeared in short order, although I didn't see who actually ate it. It could have been the blackbirds or raccoons feasting, but I continued to put it out, just in case. I was determined that no animal in need would go hungry while I had anything to say about it.

I saw her again one afternoon, but she ran from me, as usual. I warmed some canned pet food and set it beneath a tree. I retreated to the house and watched from the window as the powerful aroma enticed the cat out from hiding. She ate ravenously.

I then lined an empty cat litter box with a towel and placed it underneath the front deck. It didn't offer much protection from the elements, but I thought it would be more comfortable then the frozen ground. The cat investigated, found it to her liking, and moved in immediately. From that day on, she lived under my porch and I continued to feed her daily.

I made her a more substantial home out of a cardboard box completely lined with carpet on the inside, and plastic on the outside to repel moisture. In spite of the bitter cold, she preferred the open box to the sheltered one. It wasn't until after she had torn away some of the front and side panels of the enclosed box that she began to sleep in it regularly. I realized from her actions that protection from the snow and wind wasn't enough; she also needed to assess her surroundings visually. Her sense of security was dependent on her ability to escape quickly from predators and other dangers.

She soon recognized me as her benefactress and would rush to greet me. She allowed me to pet her head and, in time, to hold her for brief periods. She purred affectionately, but our relationship was strictly on her terms.

Our increasing closeness allowed me to discover that she was quite thin. It was only the fluffiness of her thick winter coat, which she kept remarkably clean, that had prevented me from realizing how near starvation she had been. Closer inspection revealed the white fur to be tipped with orange highlights. That, and her blue eyes, marked her as a Flamepoint Siamese. She had apparently been struggling to survive on her own for most of her young life. She was fiercely independent, but still had kittenish desires for play and comfort.

I needed to call the cat something, but I didn't want the familiarity of actually naming her. I didn't plan on keeping her; my intention was to socialize her, then find her a permanent home. I figured that her new caretakers, whoever they might be, would give her a proper name.

I already had two small dogs, and that was enough. My previous cats had died some years before, and while I missed the unique qualities that feline friends bring to a household, I had promised my mother, with whom I shared the house, that I wouldn't acquire any more cats. My mother considered cats to be good for nothing except destroying furniture, shedding and malodorous catboxes. I didn't share her concerns, but a promise is a promise. I simply referred to the cat as "Kitty."

Kitty materialized instantly whenever I went outside. She was eager for company and viewed every activity as an adventure. She "helped" me shovel the snow from the driveway, scattering it about as she frolicked. The back-breaking chore became fun when I viewed it freshly through her eyes.

If I had the dogs with me, as I often did, Kitty studied them intently. The dogs, for the most part, ignored her. It was Kitty who made the first overtures, approaching them cautiously and tentatively touching noses. Wilbur, my black terrier, dismissed her as being unworthy of his attention. Brittany, a white Lhasa Apso, was stimulated by Kitty's boldness. Brittany would kick her hind legs and bark, inviting Kitty to play. Unfamiliar with canine body language, Kitty interpreted the invitation as aggression and scampered away, only to try her charms again later.

I discovered that Kitty had excellent hunting skills, honed by necessity, I'm sure. I started finding clumps of feathers, and occasionally I caught her in the act. I understood that she was only being true to her nature, and her God-given instincts had enabled her to survive. I was saddened, though, especially since I was an unwilling accomplice.

One of my daily chores was to distribute food for the wildlife. Kitty accompanied me on my rounds as I filled the feeders and stuck peanuts in tree niches. She thought this was marvelous. She viewed it as inspired teamwork—I would attract the birds and she would dispatch them! What a wonderful idea! Naturally, I didn't agree. I tried reasoning with her, explaining that other creatures needed to eat, just as she did, and now that her food was provided freely, I expected her to respect the mealtimes of others and to let them forage in peace. She was unpersuaded by my logic, but I got the last word in—I bought her a bell collar.

Although I didn't exactly win the argument, we did reach a compromise. I rearranged the location and height of the feeders, and the bell gave the animals fair warning. Her success rate plummeted, but her efforts did not. She relentlessly stalked any and all life forms. She was no longer driven to fill an empty stomach, but still enjoyed the act of conquest. She was thrilled when she knocked a squirrel off the fence. Watching it do an involuntary double somersault as it was catapulted into the air, and its shriek of alarm, was victory enough for her.

As she became more familiar with the dogs, they, too, were fair game. She would hide under the porch or car and wait for the opportune moment to spring out and surprise them. Brittany would rear back, looking bewildered by the sneak attack, and Wilbur growled under his breath, undoubtedly muttering the canine equivalent of "What's your problem?"

Inanimate objects were equally targeted for attack. It could be a leaf, rock or twig. Anything could catch her fancy and she would wriggle with anticipation, leaping and pouncing on the unwitting item. I was reminded of how, as a child in a poor family with little money to spare for toys, I happily played with spools of thread and my mother's curlers, for hours on end. It just goes to show that it really doesn't take money or expensive toys to amuse oneself—the proper use of imagination can turn anything into entertainment.

By December, the snow was piled high and the frigid temperatures kept me inside as much as possible. Kitty would stand on the woodbox just outside the front door and peer in through the living room window. She'd tap her paw on the glass to get our attention, as if the intensity of her gaze wasn't enough. I repeatedly invited her inside, but she was hesitant to enter unfamiliar territory. She would come just inside the front entryway, but as soon as I closed the door, she panicked. As long as I left the door open a crack, she would sit and observe.

Occasionally she would make tentative forays farther into the room or into the adjacent kitchen. It was obvious that she had never been inside of a house before. Everything startled her: the hum of the refrigerator, voices on the television, inadvertently brushing against furniture—every new experience sent her fleeing back to the exit. She was brave and confident outside, in spite of the very real dangers of coyotes and cars. Inside, she was nothing more than, well, a scaredy-cat.

If I could introduce her to indoor living, it would be easier to find her a home, but her insistence on having the door open made these exploratory sessions brief. Chill air blew through the house, and a rising heat bill demanded that she make a choice—in or out. I could tell that she enjoyed the temporary reprieve from the harsh weather, but possible entrapment in alien surroundings posed too much of a risk, to her way of thinking. Back outside she would go, only to take up her perch on the woodbox, and stare at us longingly.

The nights were long, but the days were filled with excitement. She was queen of a frozen jungle, and spent her days stalking anything that moved. Her presence was occasionally challenged by Sassy, a neighbor's Siamese cat, who resented Kitty's infringement on what had formerly been, according to Sassy, an extension of her own domain. Sassy declared war on Kitty and would chase her across the street. Sassy then ambled smugly back through my yard, quite satisfied with herself. Hours later, when the coast was clear, Kitty would return and resume the hunt.

She often scrambled up trees in pursuit of her prey. Getting down was not as easy as climbing up, and one particular tree conveniently grew near the second-floor balcony. With minimal effort, Kitty found that she could jump from the tree to the balcony. She was on firm footing once again, but still had the perplexing problem of getting back to the ground.

I took this opportunity to "rescue" her. She gratefully let me pick her up, but became tense as I carried her indoors. She clung to me tenaciously as I paused in every room to let her look around and see for herself that we weren't hiding any monsters upstairs. We proceeded downstairs where I showed her the remaining rooms that she had still been too hesitant to explore. I then deposited her back outside where she still felt more secure.

She became increasingly more courageous during her inside visits, venturing farther into the house for longer periods of time. One evening she allowed me to close the door behind her without protest. I turned off the lights and went to bed, leaving her to fend for herself in the wilderness of our home.

I awoke the next morning to find Kitty staring at me from the floor. I don't know if she slept or remained vigilant throughout the night, but she was none the worse for wear. We went outside and Kitty promptly relieved herself, along with the dogs, proving herself to be a considerate houseguest.

Kitty remained outside for the day, while the dogs and I returned inside to open presents and celebrate Christmas. The significance of Kitty's first night in the house didn't occur to me until later. On Christmas Eve, Kitty had taken a big step towards domestication. It was a wonderful gift, indeed.

From then on, Kitty came and went as she pleased. I provided a catbox and she understood its purpose immediately. I suspect she preferred the warm, dry convenience of the catbox to burrowing through snow and frozen dirt to perform her necessities. In any case, her quick adaptation scored points with my mother.

Kitty soon discovered other enchantments of indoor living. Foremost among these were heat vents. She would hover above one, pawing at it in an effort to goad it into action. Eventually her efforts would pay off and the warm air would magically blow forth, to her delight. Further discoveries included pens and papers, which she decided belong on the floor. She made it her personal mission to correct my error in judgment by constantly sweeping them off my desk for me, and hiding them for good measure. She was also enamored of towels, wrestling them into submission and licking them affectionately. When she tired of these activities, there was always her tail to contend with. She would chase it endlessly, often spinning her way up and down the stairs or rattling the kitchen cabinets in her frenzy.

The dogs found Kitty's irrepressible behavior disturbing to their senior sensibilities, but she didn't lack for playmates. Admirers lined up outside for her attention. Up until then, I wasn't entirely sure of her gender, but it was quickly apparent that her new friends were gentlemen callers, and obnoxious ones at that. They wailed and howled at all hours, and even had the audacity to hiss at me when I whisked the object of their affection inside and tried to shoo them away. Arrangements were made as soon as possible to have Kitty spayed.

The appointed day came and I took her to the vet. I thought a day of peace and quiet might be nice, a respite from Kitty's boundless energy and wild ways. I was wrong. "It feels like something's missing, don't you think?" I said to my mother. "It feels dull and lifeless around here."

"Mmmm," she replied, noncommittally.

Within days, Kitty had recovered from her surgery. It was time to find her a home. I had no sooner returned from putting up flyers when I received a phone call inquiring about the cat up for adoption. At first I was thrilled; I very much wanted Kitty to have a good home. I talked to the woman on the phone for nearly an hour, with growing trepidation.

The stranger told me her history with cats; most of them had died at a young age, seemingly of neglect. She told me how pleased she was that the cat was already spayed, as she couldn't afford to have it done. How, I wondered, would she pay for a vet bill if the need arose?

She answered vaguely, then spoke to me of how she didn't believe in indiscriminate breeding when so many animals languished unwanted in pounds, yet she currently had a pregnant dog and had formerly bred dogs for profit for years. I found myself trying to talk her out of wanting the cat, pointing out the expense and commitment involved. She remained firm in her desire and in the end I agreed to deliver the cat the following day.

I hung up, still feeling uneasy. The conversation echoed in my head; the woman had contradicted herself so many times that half of what she told me amounted to lies. She had sometimes slurred her words, as if alcohol lubricated her tongue. How could I give this innocent cat to a woman of questionable character? I knew it was wrong. I would be betraying the cat's trust in me that I had worked so hard to earn.

I believed that God had brought Kitty to me for a reason, knowing that I would care for His creature in need. In return, she brought a lively joyfulness to the household. I felt that God would be deeply disappointed if I rejected the gift He'd entrusted to me. Yet I had promised my mother, and I had to respect her feelings.

My mother came into the room as tears of conflict streamed from my eyes. "Call that woman back," she said. "Tell her the cat already has a good home."

Nearly a year has passed now and Kitty is a full-fledged family member. Even Kitty's old nemesis, Sassy, has grudgingly accepted her. We were all in the backyard, and had been for several minutes, when Sassy suddenly darted out from under the shed. Kitty took off running, with Sassy in hot pursuit and, just as suddenly, Sassy was fleeing in the opposite direction, being chased by the dogs.

Kitty watched the change in circumstances with avid interest. Her attitude was "Yeah—way to go! These are my dogs. You mess with me and you're messing with my dogs. And don't you forget it!"

The formerly unwanted cat has another unexpected ally; my mother spoils her, lavishing her with store-bought lunch meats and performing doorman duties at Kitty's whim, without complaint. My mother always has been partial to white animals. I think God knew that, too.

A True Friendship

LYNN SEELY

 wondered if I would see the fawn or her unusual companion this morning. I heard a light patter on the window that announced my favorite weather had arrived. I loved running in the rain. Once outside, I fell into the slow, steady stride that would be easy to maintain for miles. The gentle sprinkle muffled my footsteps. Since asthma and dusty country roads don't mix, I had avoided my favorite route for the past few days—but not this morning.

The oppressive dust that had covered everything was gone, creating new visions of familiar scenery. Trees bent slightly as temporary jewels shimmered on each leaf. Puddles offered invitations to the hesitant droplets, beckoning them to skydive. Crystal creeks splashed cool greetings, gurgling happily across ancient rocks and smooth boulders. I came to a forest of cedars, immense and ancient, their great branches murmuring secrets as I passed by. I wondered what they had been witness to over years. They seemed to speak of quiet dignity and calmness and were living proof that even though storms may come, it is possible to survive most of them. This summer as the sun beat down upon me, they had offered silent relief. Today they granted me serene refuge from the chaos of the world, a tunnel of tranquillity to run through.

A short while later, I arrived at my special place. I always stopped here before returning home. The rain had stopped. The air was heavy with the perfume of cedar and pine. A nearby meadow—where the fawn sometimes appeared—was sparkling in the dim morning light. Smoky mist drifted gently skyward from a small lake. Beyond that a distant mountain, no longer wearing the dull mantle of dust, glistened clean and pristine. I stepped off the road and made my way over to a fallen log. The ground was carpeted with emerald green moss; a living velvet that made everything it draped soft and inviting. Moss covered the very bottom of the log, while the top was bare wood. It made a perfect seat.

Birds serenaded me with their morning songs and invited me to experience their enthusiastic joy. Some were using puddles to bath in, their vigorous splashing and preening left no doubt they were relieved that the long drought was over. I noticed fresh tracks in the cow-brown earth. They were strange-looking tracks and I could only speculate about what had made them. A hawk passed low overhead, but it had been so silent and disappeared so quickly into the gray mist that I wondered if I had imagined it.

So far, I had not seen any deer this morning, but when I had encountered them previously, they always seem astonished at my presence. I have laughed out loud at the expressions on their faces. They are not afraid of me, but they do seem amazed that a lumbering human would do such a thing as run! They often show me what true grace is as they wheel about and silently bound up a mountainside or across a grassy meadow.

I was ready to return home when I saw her. The little fawn was walking carefully, ears twitching for any sound that could mean danger. I froze, not wanting to startle her. She had beautiful brown eyes, and dappled white spots still covered her tawny coat. She was too young to be without her mother—yet it was clear she was. Her mother would have spotted me easily. This fawn was still inexperienced and she had not yet learned the lessons she needed to survive. As delighted as I was to see her, I worried about her.

Suddenly her companion appeared. The next instant, a piercing squawk filled the air again and again. The fawn's friend happens to be a large black crow! I had seen them together on three separate occasions, and it was always the same. The crow filled the air with penetrating alerts. The fawn stiffened for a moment—her tawny ears twitching nervously—as she searched for danger. She still did not see me. The crow hopped across the branches and came closer to me as it continued to pierce the air with urgent warnings. The fawn turned toward the crow. She finally saw me and wheeled about, her white tail a flag of alarm. In an instant she was gone.

The crow stayed only a few moments longer and got in a few more reproving screeches before it flew off in the direction the fawn had taken. I was finally convinced that the crow and fawn were together. I smiled. The fawn wasn't alone after all. She had a friend. Indeed, though I had to admit it was a strange one for a fawn to have, the crow was a good friend nonetheless.

I recalled a lone crow I had noticed the year before. For some reason it seemed to be an outcast from the flock of crows that frequented the area. In fact, I saw them chase him away time and time again. As I witnessed this pathetic scene, I felt sorry that the crow was not allowed to stay. Of course, I could not say for certain that this was the same crow, but I thought it might be. If so, perhaps it was lonely because of the rejection of the flock and had somehow connected with the little motherless fawn . Maybe the fawn had bleated for its mother and when she did not appear, the crow had responded in an effort to console it or warn it of danger. Speculation aside, the fact was that they had somehow struck up this special friendship.

It was time for me to leave and I decided to return home a different way than I had come. A short while later I reached the top of a very steep hill. I paused for a while and gazed out at the vast miles of creation stretched before me. A mountain range lay in the distance, shrouded in swirling mist. The early morning sun was sending streamers of golden light dancing across the eastern slopes of the mountain nearest me as well as across the neatly cropped corn fields that stood silent and empty.

Well—almost empty. To my amazement, there in the cornfield, walking side by side were the little fawn and the crow! Although the corn stalks had already been harvested, pieces of discarded corn littered the ground. The fawn and the crow were making their way across the field, eating. It was a tender, remarkable sight, one that I knew I would never forget. It was a picture of true friendship.

215

The Something That Went Thump in the Night

RENIE SZILAK BURGHARDT

 I was eleven when we arrived in the refugee camp in Austria, after having fled our war-torn country, Hungary, in 1947. The camp, located on the outskirts of a small town, was dismal, but at least all our immediate needs were taken care of, and we were grateful to the Lord for that.

The people who ran the camp set up a school for the children, and organized a Scout group. Soon I was a Girl Scout, and even went to a Scout camp that summer, held in the beautiful Tyrol region of Austria.

The camp, located in the wooded mountains outside the village of Alm, was quite a nice set-up. On one side of a clear, rushing creek were the tents for the girls and our troop leader, Mrs. Kovacs. On the other side, the boys and Mr. Kovacs, the other troop leader, were camping out. But it was on the boy's side where we all went for our meals, and for the nightly campfire that was held there as well.

These campfires were always the highlight at the end of the day. We girls, with Mrs. Kovacs, would cross the little bridge that went over the creek and join the boys around the fire, singing songs, telling stories, and playing games. All—beneath those beautiful, tall, whispering pine trees that covered the entire area—had a wonderful time.

216

To teach us courage and responsibility, I guess, our two troop leaders soon decided on a plan. Every night, while the rest of the troop trekked across the bridge to the boy's side, for the campfire, one girl would stay behind as the sole guard. This girl was given a whistle, in the event she became scared and needed help of any kind, but other than that, she would be alone in the big, dark woods. If she blew the whistle, she would be heard, and help would arrive within a few minutes, the leaders told us.

Most of the girls, eleven and twelve years old, were not happy with this arrangement, but complained only to each other about it. Nevertheless, the ones who got early turns at being guards seemed to do their job well, never once blowing the whistle while sitting in the dark for 2 hours. But the stories they told later, of strange noises coming from the pitch-black woods, frightened the heebie-jeebies out of the girls who hadn't had a turn yet.

"I heard terrible grunting, and I was sure a bear was coming to eat me," a girl named Anna told us as we lay in our tent later that night.

"So why didn't you blow the whistle?" I asked, chills running up and down my spine.

"Because I didn't want everyone to call me a chicken," Anna replied. "And I'm glad I didn't. The bear went away after a while. I'm lucky he wasn't hungry."

"I heard strange noises when I was guard," another girl piped up. "It sounded like a woman crying. I even called out to her, but there was no answer. I decided it must have been a ghost, and she finally went to haunt someone else. But Mrs. Kovacs said it was probably only an owl. I still think it was a ghost."

"I wonder if there are any wolves in these woods," still another girl asked. "My turn is coming up soon."

"Mine, too," I said, "and I can tell you one thing: if I get scared, I will blow the whistle. I'd rather be called a chicken than be eaten by a wolf or bear."

So the following night, my turn to be the guard arrived. Mrs. Kovacs, one of our troop leaders, placed the whistle, hung on a long string, around my neck, and handed me a flashlight.

"Remember, we'll be just across the creek. If you get scared, blow this whistle," she said, smiling at me. The other girls glanced back as they walked away, glad it wasn't their turn. Then they were all gone.

I sat down on a campstool in front of my tent, my heart already pounding way too fast, butterflies doing a jig in my stomach. I could see the campfire across the creek, and hear the distant singing voices. Everything would be all right, I told myself, glancing uneasily around the now pitch-dark camp and woods. The other girls survived their two hours as guards, and so would I.

I looked up above the towering pines, and saw some stars and a crescent moon in the sky. I inhaled the wonderful smell of the pines. I began to relax and feel quite good. This wasn't so bad. In fact, it was nice to be alone, in the quiet woods, I decided, and began humming a little tune to entertain myself.

Then it happened. I heard a noise. A very loud thump! Thump! Then it stopped. "Who's there?" I called out. I heard a rustle, followed by more thumps, getting louder and louder. This wasn't my imagination playing tricks on me, there was something or someone out there, and it was heading my way! It couldn't be a wolf, I thought right away; a wolf would sneak up without all that thumping. It had to be a bear, and it was getting too close for comfort. Then, just when I was ready to blow the whistle, the huge thumper of the night came into my view, and stood there right in front of me. I shined my flashlight on him.

"Snort! Snort!" went the thumper, bobbing his head up and down.

"You're a horse!" I shrieked, spitting the whistle out of my mouth. "A big, giant horse! Hello there, boy, where did you come from?" I held out my hand as I talked to him. The horse's muzzle touched my fingers. He snorted again. I boldly reached up and patted his head gently.

"There, there, boy. You must be lost or something. I'm sure they'll find your owner in the morning. Meanwhile, you can keep me company, since I don't like to be alone in the dark," I said, as I continued patting him. "Actually, I think my guardian angel must have sent you my way, just so I wouldn't be so scared."

The horse snorted again. I wondered if I had something in the tent I could give him as a treat.

"You wait here, I'll be right back," I told him, creeping into the tent and feeling around. "Here it is, a box of keks that I saved. I think you'll like these, boy." Keks were a kind of cookie/cracker combination that

was really popular in Austria at the time, and we had each received a packet of them in case we got hungry between meals.

The horse did, indeed, like the keks, and wanted more and more. Soon my package was empty. I walked around the camp boldly now, my companion right behind me the entire time. Noises I heard no longer frightened me. I had a guardian with me. I was actually sorry to hear voices crossing the creek, as the others were returning.

"Look, Mrs. Kovacs, I had company tonight," I called out to them. "So I wasn't alone at all."

"A horse! Look, girls, Renie has a horse with her," one of the girls shrieked excitedly, as a whole bunch of girls gathered around my companion and me.

"Where did he come from?" "I wonder whose horse he is?" "Weren't you frightened when he came?" And many other questions followed. Mrs. Kovacs then blew the whistle, and her husband, from the boy's side, came running across the creek.

"Probably belongs to the farm nearby. We'll check with the farmer

219

in the morning," Mr. Kovacs said, going back to get a rope. "We'll tie him to a tree for tonight."

Well, the following morning some boys went to the farm, and it turned out that the horse had gotten out from the pasture and galloped through the woods. Until he found me, that is!

"I had a horse just like this one in Hungary," I told the farmer when he came to get my companion. "I used to ride him all the time. Then we had to sell him because of the war."

"Well," he said, "you can come and ride Rudy while you're here. He's pretty gentle, and he really seems to like you."

And that's what I did. I went to ride Rudy several times before we went back to the refugee camp, and all the other girls considered me the bravest of the guards for not blowing my whistle when I heard a thump in the pitch-dark night!

A Quail of a Story

ART LIENHART

ne day in the late summer of 1999 I was bush-hogging a six-acre pasture for a friend. I had completed several loops around the pasture when a male quail came out of the tall grass and stopped about 20 feet from the tractor. I immediately stopped the tractor and turned off the engine.

First I must tell you that I talk to animals as if they were part of the family, and sometimes you might be surprised at what they will do.

I knew what the quail was trying to tell me, and I began talking to him. I asked him several times to call the female out where I could see her so I wouldn't run over her. Nothing happened, so I started the tractor and proceeded mowing the pasture in first gear and looking for the female. After a few hundred feet, I increased speed.

I made two more loops around the pasture, and each time I came back to that same spot, there was the male, just standing there. Each time I turned off the engine and talked to him, but the female never appeared. I knew she was in the tall grass, so I mowed very slowly.

On the third loop, still moving slowly, I saw the female at the edge of the tall grass. Immediately I stopped and turned off the engine. Following behind the female were 14 small baby quails, the last four

221

barely able to maneuver through the grass. Then I started to talk to the female. As I walked to the front of the tractor, I was looking in the tall grass for any babies that might be having problems.

I was less than 10 feet from the female when the male appeared. I started talking to both of them, telling them they had a pretty family and to take care of the babies. The whole time I was talking to them, they just stood there looking at me as if they understood every word I said. Then I went back to the tractor, started the engine and continued mowing the pasture. As I went by the family, they didn't move, knowing that I wouldn't harm them. When I completed the next loop, the family was nowhere to be found.

Four or five days later, I had to mow a different part of the same property. I was approaching a burn pile when I noticed the male and female quail and all fourteen babies next to the pile. I stopped the tractor and talked to them again, explaining that they were in the tractor's way. Again, they stood still and seemed to listen. Then they led the babies over to a safe place and I continued with the mowing.

Two weeks later, I was mowing the pasture again. For some reason I looked to the right, and less than 20 feet from the tractor were the male and female in flight, going as slowly as they could. About 20 feet behind them were the babies, all 14 of them, in flight. They crossed over in front of me and landed in the corner of the pasture and waited for me.

I drove the tractor within 15 feet of the family, and nobody moved. I talked to them and told them again that they had a pretty family and to take good care of the babies. The female turned around, went through the fence, followed by the babies, one and two at a time. When the last baby was through the fence, the male stood there for a few more seconds. then he turned and went through the fence.

I have never seen more than two quail in flight at one time—yet here was a family of sixteen that survived the raising of a family and said "Thank you" with a fly-by.

Question: Do wild animals understand what you say or do? You be the judge.

Robbie's Legacy

RAY McDONALD

he signs of spring were everywhere. The grass was lush green. The birds were announcing a new day. The early morning mist made the cows look wraithlike as they grazed in the nearby pasture.

I wiped the dew from one of my deck chairs and sipped my first cup of coffee while watching the world awaken. The breeze loosened the last of a flowering pear tree's blossoms and floated them to the ground like big oval snowflakes. Amid this serenity a male robin was hard at work. He was building a nest in the all-too-young and fragile pear tree which had been planted only a season before. It was growing about ten feet from my deck. He worked with an urgency that told me his mate would soon present him with a son or daughter—or both.

His structure was not to be a small, one-room, walk-up efficiency. My feathered friend fancied himself the Frank Lloyd Wright of birdland. Judging from the materials he lifted to a height some twelve feet from the ground, he intended building an aviary mansion. I rose and tried to scare the bird off to a less precarious spot, but the ten feet of air space between us gave him a sense of security. He gave two chirps and fluttered his wings as if to tell me to mind my own business, then went back to work. I went back to my chair and my coffee.

Two mornings later I looked from my deck to see the nest occupied by Mrs. Robin. I so informed my wife, Mary Jo. Now if Saint Francis of Assisi has a present-day, female counterpart, it is Mary Jo. She delights in all creatures and is a willing midwife at birthing time. She examined the nest and pronounced it insecure and also pronounced me delinquent for not informing her sooner. She would await the opportune moment to anchor the nest firmly. Father Robin had formed his foundation well but the small tree was unprotected from the gusty winds that whistle across our quadrangle-shaped development.

The situation became grave when Mary Jo found a single pale-blue egg in the nest the following morning. Mother, I suppose, had gone shopping. Mary Jo used her absence to secure the dwelling with fishing line. Now if she could only find a way to keep the egg in place when the wind bent the sapling close to the ground. She prayed for calm weather.

If you have seen the wide eyes and sparkling smile of a child who has just received a new puppy, then you know something of the look on Mary Jo's face the morning she checked the nest and found not an egg but a live baby bird whose open, yellow-rimmed beak was wider than its fuzz-covered, pink body. The first hurdle was cleared.

A steady train of well-wishers, old and young, used the deck's vantage point to view the new arrival. This maternity ward had a large viewing area.

Then came the wind. The little pear tree was bent like a tall palm in a typhoon. Robbie's house was tossed about like a rowboat in a tempest. Mary Jo gasped as she watched the little guy topple the twelve feet to the ground. She rushed to his aid. He labored to breathe. She gently returned him to the nest. It isn't true that birds abandon their young if there is human contact. Mr. and Mrs. Robin witnessed all of my wife's actions, yet returned to their baby.

The winds were not finished. On the following day Robbie was tossed from his home three times. Each fall was thought fatal, but somehow the little guy survived. The final fall brought part of the nest to the earth. Now Robbie could not be returned to the tree, and the parents could no longer care for their offspring. Since he had no nest, to leave him on the ground would place him in harm's way from predators. Decision time...Mary Jo gathered the larger pieces of the broken nest, placed the little bird on them as if it were a bed and carefully carried him inside.

What Robbie needed now was TLC. What Mary Jo needed was advice. A neighbor, Mary Le Master, was the first on hand. She had no expertise but had a friend who did. She left a message for a biology teacher at the local college (Shepherd) and marked the call urgent. Mary Jo called the Audubon Society. While awaiting the return calls Mary Jo located her smallest eyedropper. I was assigned the duty of observing the little guy. I watched the small body heave as he struggled with each breath. His injuries did not seem to affect his appetite. We were successful with the eyedropper. Our calls were returned. After learning the bird's age, the professor suggested rolling lean ground beef into the form of a worm. Robbie took to it like a kid with a McDonald's Happy Meal. The Audubon Society confirmed our practices as correct and added the suggestion of making a thick mush of dry dog food and rolling it in the same fashion. Robbie liked this, too. Each night Mary Jo would check our charge and each morning I would see if Robbie had survived the night. On the fifth morning, the tiny bird lay still.

I gave Robbie a proper burial in a garden where life is continually renewed. As I smoothed the earth over his wee body I reflected upon how many lives were affected by this creature's short visit. This story might suitably end here...but it doesn't.

Another spring is "Bustin' Out All Over." In the country the bird chirps signal the sunrise or perhaps the first rays ignite the chirps. The breeze whispers through my pear tree and I think I shall hear the leaves tinkle like sleigh bells. The tractor hum will soon follow...such wonderful music to open a beautiful celestial symphony.

Now Robins don't wear nameplates, but I would swear that the same builder has constructed a home on the corner of my deck. This time he has taken no chances with the fragile trees. He and the Missus have decided to become patients of Dr. Mary Jo early on. This time Mom has laid not one but three pale blue eggs. They have all hatched. Mary Jo has given encouragement and even helped with the shopping. Almost overnight the baby fuzz has magically turned to feathers. Unlike the tree with its water-repellent foliage, the deck provides no protection from the hard rains. Ours may be the only nest with its own umbrella.

It is almost time for the three would-be flyers to solo. Our world will have a little more beauty. What's in this for me? I get to see that radiant look on Mary Jo's face. No wonder Saint Francis is always pictured with a smile.

Saying Goodbye

And God shall wipe away

all tears from their eyes...

(Revelation 21:4, KJV).

The Cat Who Came Back

CAROL WALLACE

e didn't need another cat. When a friend dropped by with a tiny white kitten in search of a home, we determined to be adamant. No more cats.

This one looked around calmly, not at all intimidated by the two cats (one vastly pregnant) glaring at her from their separate corners. Then she yawned, climbed up onto my husband's lap and into the pouch of his hooded sweatshirt, and fell fast asleep.

It was love at first sight. We named her Olivia.

She was a skinny thing, with bright blue eyes. As I was accustomed to black cats, she seemed to me like the ghost of a cat—but far too lively to be anything but real.

She had a flair for satire.

We fed her what we thought was a generous quantity of food. She lapped it up, then tottered weakly to the kitchen carpet, making sure we were paying attention. She then threw herself onto her back, one paw flung limply over her forehead like some cinema tragedy queen and mewed pitifully. We brought her more food.

My husband went to feed the dog. I heard laughter as he opened that 50 pound bag, and he called me to come look. There was Olivia, reclining casually on the dog food pellets, taking a languid munch or two as the spirit moved her. It became one of her favorite resting places.

Once fed, she gave us an after-dinner show, a vigorous tail-chasing that we came to anticipate. A natural clown, she loved to provoke laughter. Even Peabody and Nell came to watch.

Olivia approached everyone and everything with ears up and forward—classic cat language for friendliness. She radiated love to everyone and everything without reserve, seeming to have no clue about the darker sides of life. Love and you will be loved was her motto. It worked.

Even the most curmudgeonly of creatures—my cat Nell—loved her back. I often came upon them: a fluffy bit of white sleeping soundly, with the paranoid and usually hostile Nell curled protectively around her.

When Peabody had her kittens under our bed, I peeked—and saw four tiny grey-and-black kittens and one larger white one suckling peacefully. Peabody only yawned.

More times than I can count, cat haters found themselves sitting and talking, unaware that they had been stroking a little white cat. Like a set of worry beads, she offered the comfort of repetitive stroking motions and soft, soothing sounds, so unobtrusively that those receiving her therapy were not aware of it.

In the garden I was Olivia's shade tree. She also lingered beneath a small, weeping Japanese maple that was just her size and which didn't keep moving as I did. She would inspect my work, make scary faces at birds using the feeder, then nudge me in search of some quality time. She was my white shadow and furry clown, lightening the monotony of endless weeding.

That last day she stuck close to my side, taking brief side trips to greet the other cats, the wheelbarrow, or anything else she could bestow some affection on. It was scorching, and we rested frequently, she snuggled under the crook of my knee as if it were a parasol. The heat encouraged more resting than working—and so there was lots of quality time.

I'm glad.

Because the next day as I drove down the street on my way to class I saw something white and still through the rain pouring down my windshield, and I stopped.

She lay in a huge running puddle of water, almost as if asleep—except that one of her beautiful blue eyes had burst from its socket.

I forgot the car, forgot everything, and started up the hill with her in my arms, tears and rain mingling as I spoke to her—praying for even a sign of life, yet knowing it was futile. Olivia had bounded toward a car with love—but this time it didn't love her back.

I covered her with a scrap of velvet and waited for my husband. I wouldn't let him look—that eye hanging from its socket had traumatized me, robbed me of Olivia's beauty.

We buried her beneath her little Japanese maple, weeping harder than the skies. We couldn't eat that night, even speak much, except for the occasional angry word that fell from my husband's lips. I tried to remember the laughter our little clown-cat brought, but all I could see was that dangling eye.

Nell and Peabody declared a truce; they sat with me or prowled about, mewing, looking for their "little white thing." We huddled together until I heard a thump of frightening magnitude outside the window. Both cats' fur stood on end.

I wasn't surprised to see a cat shape in the window—all of mine thump on it if they want to come inside. But Nell and Peabody were with me—and the cat in the window was white.

I went closer. She looked at me, with eyes bright, blue—and perfect. Her bright pink collar still displayed its tiny antique silver cat charm. My mind denied it, but my eyes inspected every detail.

It was Olivia. A perfect, peaceful, beautiful Olivia.

She sat quietly, turning her head a bit so that I could see both eyes intact. I begged her to wait so I could open the door. If she had looked like a ghost cat to me in life, she seemed very much alive in that window. But when I opened the door, she was gone.

My husband was skeptical at first. But we knew that Olivia's role in our lives had been as clown and as comforter. And we needed comfort. So she came back for a moment, to show us that in that other world that few of us understand, she was whole and happy. Then she left for good.

But years later, her memory still brings smiles.

Tidings of Comfort

EVELYN BENCE

ast week I dreamt that for much of a workday a maned lion slept outside my home-office window, in the yard. Toward dinnertime, the lion awoke, stretched, and walked and sniffed the grass. I went out, ventured a reach toward and then into the mane. While I was still petting, or after—I don't know—the Lassie-like lion disappeared into thin air, poof! Yet I continued to sense the friendly, powerful protection and later saw the lion peering out from under a picnic table, watchful but partially hidden.

The next morning, stepping into my writer's office, my spirit was unusually peaceful, sensing the presence and blessing of that silent lion, maybe the Lion of Judah, maybe Dollie, my chief childhood comforter.

My childhood was eased by two great comforts: my dog by day and my stuffed bunny by night. I don't remember receiving the rabbit; as far as I knew, he always was. Even now, the cotton bunny watches me sleep, sitting in a doll's highchair beside my bed. His black plastic eyes and pink nose have fared better than his cloth body. On some shameful day, Mother put him in the laundry and let him spin until all his innards coagulated in his extremities, there to lump forever.

And he now has a new friend who caught my eye several years ago at a consignment shop. It may have been Mother's last visit to my home in Virginia. As was often the case, she had no money on her. With uncharacteristic boldness, she did not ask but told Dad to lay down three dollars for a nonessential purchase; she had seen my wistful smile as I stroked the face and floppy ears of a furry white bunny with black plastic eyes and a pink nose. "Buy it for her," she said. He did.

So alongside his new friend, the silent night-watch bunny that slept with me as a child is with me, with me still.

But the flesh-and-blood collie dog, she is a different story. I clearly remember the afternoon she entered my life. Five years old, I was summoned to the grand archway between the living room and dining area. Being in on the secret, my five older siblings hung back. This was my moment, my gift, though I'm sure it was meant for all.

Through the kitchen, my dad walked in, a large cardboard box held tight between his pot-belly and his thick hands. He set the box down in front of me, open side up, and there I stood nose to nose with a squirming, blonde, white-collared collie pup who licked my cheek.

Just thinking about that first greeting gives me goose bumps. I named her Dollie. It was the only day she was ever allowed in our parsonage house. Like the preceding family dogs, by Mother's decree she lived in the backyard or roamed the neighborhood, except when confined because of winter cold or passionate heat; then she was moved into the small detached garage wedged between the frame house and the stucco church.

The older children had fed and combed and mourned a black cocker and a brown collie named Thistle. My father wanted a dog on the premises. For his kids to play with? Yes. To teach them responsibility? Yes. To ease his nostalgia for the animals "down home" on his father's Pennsylvania farm? Yes. To watch out for and protect his family? Yes. Yes.

1952, the winter I was born, Thistle's incessant barking in the garage woke the family at 2 A.M. Smoke. Flames. The garage was on fire and the back side of the house singed. If not for Thistle, the house would have burned, and who knows our family's fate. Thistle suffered on her back a baseball-sized burn, which Dad rubbed with salve that healed the sore but couldn't erase the wound.

Thistle survived the fire but not the winter. My older sisters have warm stories about the black cocker who eased their loss, but I hardly remember her. Once she jumped into my arms, I championed Dollie, looking as she did like heroic Thistle, but even more like famed Lassie. It was a shame that Dollie never had pups, as she was such a mother, and not just to me. When my toddler brother, Phil, playing in the yard, ventured toward the road, Dollie blocked him with her bulk and nudged him with her nose: Back where you belong, boy!

In time I was the one who drew her water and filled her tin-can bowl with a cupful of fragrant dog chow supplemented by table scraps and sometimes beef bones. In the spring I combed her clean of a winter's overgrowth. In family outdoor photos, she's at my side, my hand buried in her coat. Approaching adolescence, when I was sure my father and mother had forsaken their tenderness toward me, my dog was there to take me up.

In sixth grade, the year Kennedy was shot, the year I was told we were moving away in the summer, the last year before my next-oldest sister left—like all the others before her—for college, Dollie was the friend who sat and listened. In July we moved to a farm; Dollie now had open access to a large barn, and any number of rodents had access to our house. For the first and only time in her life, Mother said we could have cats.

After a round of testy sniffs and spats, Dollie and the cat hung out like old blonde pals. But the cat having four kittens, nested in straw stored out in the barn, threw Dollie into a maternal crisis. Dollie, now ten years old, had never had pups; not to be denied this birthright, she claimed the kittens as hers. She licked them head to toe, nudged them to her dry belly, and carried them—the scruff of their necks clutched between her teeth—to her favorite bed. Then the cat would take them back. Then the dog. For several days you never quite knew where the kittens might be nestled with whom.

And then it happened. We'd been away all day, and when we drove into the driveway, I sensed something was wrong. Dollie was in the yard, alone, sulking. The cat wasn't in sight. I went to the gray barn, to find the kittens.

Two were dead, a third was dazed, and the fourth was milking its mother. The conflicted mothers had obviously fought it out. And Dollie had lost.

Dollie never again went near the kittens. Nor did she ever recover the vigor of her youth. If dogs age seven life-years to our one, she was, by this time, seventy and slowing. Lame with arthritis, fat with lack of exercise, she slept most of the day in the shade of the picnic table out back. That summer, running my hand across her rump, I discovered open sores on her skin, which Dad cleaned and smeared with salve but never healed.

That summer we moved again, to a house with a small yard on a city street. And that summer Dad decided that Dollie wouldn't be happy in the city, that she should be put out of her misery, that she deserved a peaceful parting and burial in the pasture behind the barn. Dad negotiated this with us by buying a cinder-black cocker pup a few months before we moved.

I was sixteen when I hugged Dollie's neck and said good-bye. Cinder, the black cocker, eased my loss, but never stole my heart. In a few years I went off to college, and Cinder was sent off to a country bachelor preacher who needed a companion to tell his troubles to.

I've never had another pet, always living in city apartments with restrictions. Nor have Mom and Dad had a pet (children grown, responsibility taught), though the roster at my mother's nursing home includes Sadie, a long-haired mutt, which Mother generally ignores. But one day this spring a nurse brought in a black cocker pup. To my sister's surprise, Mom grinned and with her good hand pulled the dog into her lap. Nose to nose, the squirming pup turned and licked her cheek. And Mother didn't pull away. For a moment she let herself delight in canine comfort, as I had as a child.

* * *

Three months have passed since I wrote this story. And two months ago my mother died. Quickly. Peacefully. Since then I've thought often of the dreamed lion—or was it a collie who thought she was an over-grown cat?—who slept in the yard all day, let me run my hand through her hair, and peered out from under a picnic table.

I want to think that in her last days my mother, with uncharacter-istic boldness, did not ask but told God to send me a comforter. By day. In the night.

One in a Million

GINA ROMSDAHL

 e was always eager to explore, from the moment he was born, pushing his way into the world first, before his brother. He was one of a litter of only two. Both he and his brother had their mother's orange tabby coloring, and it would have been impossible to tell them apart except that he was slightly bigger. I named him Igor.

Whiskey, his mother, doted on him, and he loved every minute of it. She would contentedly lick his head as he suckled her milk, and he continued to drink long after his brother had had his fill. Whiskey nursed him for four months, but eventually all good things must come to an end. Far outweighing his brother, and twice the size of his mother, Igor eventually tipped the scales at nearly thirty pounds.

Even though she no longer provided milk, Whiskey continued to provide love and care. She licked and groomed him ceaselessly, until he grew big enough to fend her off. He would bask in her attention for a short while, but her abrasive tongue would soon be more irritating than pleasurable and he would squirm out of her motherly clutches when he'd had enough.

Igor's sire, Fang, seemed to have had little influence on Igor, genetically or otherwise, except for one particular trait. Fang was a Siamese cat. His blue eyes were crossed, which must have affected his vision. Lacking in the usual feline grace, he was the klutziest cat I've ever known. For instance, once while walking in a straight path near the edge of a countertop, he strolled right into the air and fell to the floor. Such missteps were not uncommon. I'm afraid that Igor had inherited his father's propensity for them.

I had been out of town for a couple of days and left my animals in the care of a friend. When I returned, I saw Igor lying in the beanbag chair. "What's wrong with Igor?" I said.

"Nothing. What do you mean? He's fine," replied my friend.

To a casual observer, Igor would indeed look like a normal cat at rest. But when you know and love someone, be they human or animal, you can tell at a glance when something is out of the ordinary. Perhaps it's a facial expression or some subtle body language. Perhaps it's a psychic connection or an emotional bond. I knew instantly that something was wrong with Igor.

I immediately arranged to take Igor to the veterinarian's office. It turned out that he had broken one or more small bones in a front paw. Due to the tiny size and complex location of the bones, they couldn't be straightened and set individually. Instead, the vet put Igor's whole leg in a cast so that healing could at least take place without further injury.

Igor sported his cast, wrapped in a bright pink bandage, for several weeks. He was under house arrest because I feared for his safety in his impaired condition if he were to go outside. He didn't appreciate the long days of confinement, but the enforced incarceration paid off when the cast was removed and his paw was functional again, although slightly crooked. He didn't waste any time in getting back to business as usual.

For Igor, taking care of business meant maintaining his position as the dominant cat in the neighborhood hierarchy. To my dismay, Igor had a Jekyll-and-Hyde personality. The sweet cat that I knew at home, the cat that would stand on his hind legs and put both front paws around my neck and give me an affectionate hug, was also the terror of the neighborhood.

Igor had a lot of weight to throw around and he enjoyed doing so. He threatened and intimidated all other cats, except Whiskey, of course. Whiskey was Igor's mother and she never let him forget it. At home, he was submissive to her maternal authority. Outside the house was another story, however, and he commanded the respect that his size deserved. He was king of all he surveyed and he frequently patrolled the neighborhood, making sure that every feline on the block quaked in fear at his presence. Always seeking to expand his territory, he would instigate hostile takeovers. He was downright mean and nothing short of a bully.

As disagreeable as this ruthlessly savage behavior was, the other aspect of Igor's personality was that of what can only be described as a "Mama's Boy." Having been raised with two mothers, one human and one feline, he had been lavished with maternal affection for all of his born days. He reveled in it. He was, in essence, a big baby.

Whenever I would hear the familiar yowling and hissing of Igor's battles in progress, I would go outside and call him to come in. The conflict of his two natures would reveal itself in the expression on his face. He would look at me as if to say, "Oh, Mom, you're blowing my cover." He would angrily swish his tail a few times, then turn and follow me into the house. I imagined the other cats snickering behind his back, muttering comments they would never dare say to his face, such as "What a sissy!"

After one of these humiliating retreats, Igor would assert himself closer to home for a while. Ours was a two-story, A-frame house. The roof was steeply sloped to facilitate the melting of heavy winter snowfall. We had an upstairs balcony, and Whiskey often leapt onto the railing and from there to the roof where she could explore the nooks and crannies of the wooden shingles. She was dainty and graceful and accomplished this feat with ease.

One warm summer day, Igor had apparently decided that if Whiskey could do it, he could, too. I had seen him leap to the roof, with mild concern due to his inherited paternal clumsiness. His leap was successful, however, and I didn't give it another thought. A short while later I heard strange scritching noises from above. Hm-m-m. Must be a clump of pine needles sliding down, or perhaps a rolling pine cone, I thought. The noise stopped, then continued again. There was another pause, then more scrabbling noises, followed by a long whooshing sound. Alarmed, I ran to the window and looked outside where I saw Igor sitting dazed in a heap on the ground.

239

I rushed downstairs with Whiskey following closely behind me. I flung open the front door and there stood Igor, waiting to be let in. He indignantly brushed past my legs, gave Whiskey a dirty look and swatted her face, as if the incident were somehow her fault, and casually sauntered inside. He was miraculously unhurt—except, of course, for his pride.

When Igor was twelve years old, he developed a skin condition. He lost a good deal of hair along his back and hindquarters, and gained numerous little bumps, like tiny pimples. The veterinarian injected him with a steroidal drug, to be followed with more steroid pills for several days. I wasn't sure how easy it would be to pill him, so I enlisted my mother's help. I wanted her to restrain him, while I forced him to swallow the buttered tablet. As it turned out, no force was necessary. He swallowed the pill without a hitch, then promptly rolled over onto his back so that I could rub his massive belly. He loved being the center of attention, whatever the reason.

The vet had informed me that one of the side effects of the medication was excessive thirst and urination, so I wasn't surprised when these effects manifested. He was still drinking copious amounts of water two weeks after the pills had ceased. He was growing lethargic and we went back to the vet to deal with these new symptoms.

The vet now informed me that one of the rare, but possible, side effects of ingesting steroids was the inducement of diabetes in the patient. Igor's blood sugar was tested and found to be extremely high. The vet gave me more pills, this time to lower his blood sugar.

Igor was cooperative beyond my wildest dreams. I didn't have to butter the pills, or disguise them with food. I just held the pills in my hand and Igor ate them willingly. He did his part; unfortunately the pills didn't do theirs. His condition worsened and back to the vet we went.

After a twenty-four-hour series of blood tests, taken at four-hour intervals, the vet decided on a recommended level of insulin and I was allowed to take Igor home. I would give him insulin injections myself, once a day at first, and soon twice daily.

Igor was as sweet as could be, both literally and figuratively. He never resisted the needle pricks to the back of his fleshy neck. He was trusting and more affectionate than ever, yet his blood sugar remained high and he showed little response to the treatment. He was listless and weak, and fear gripped my heart as he began to waste away.

240

He lost his appetite. He was large and big-boned, but the flesh hung on his husky frame as he grew thinner and thinner. I fed him a special diet of easily digestible food that the vet had recommended. It was high in fiber to help flush the excess glucose from his system, but he couldn't eat more than a few bites at a time. He continued to drink massive amounts and I had to completely change the catbox litter at least once a day, it was that soggy.

Several months had passed and my handsome Igor was now only a shadow of his former self. He still purred when I petted him and I continued to hope for the best. Whiskey and I watched helplessly as he slid further and further away from us.

One morning I went to check on my patient and he wouldn't look at me. I moved to his other side and he turned away from me. He wouldn't meet my eyes and I knew the day had come. He was miserable. He was giving up the fight, and his refusal to make eye contact was his way of asking me to let him go.

We returned to the vet's office one last time. I gently petted Igor as we waited for the vet to administer the lethal injection. I noticed a bald spot on the top of his head that hadn't been there the day before. I thought it was odd, but the thought quickly slipped away as I dealt with the somber matter at hand. In a moment, Igor was gone. The loss was immediate and painful to me, yet I was glad for his release from suffering.

The vet requested that I allow her to do a necropsy, at no charge. Igor's case had been a puzzling one and she hoped to learn something that might aid her in treating future patients. I consented, and several weeks later I learned that Igor had been hemorrhaging from his pancreas, and was undoubtedly in much pain at the time of death.

When I returned home without Igor, Whiskey met me at the door. She seemed to know that Igor wouldn't be returning with me, and we comforted each other. As she repeatedly licked my hand, I remembered the bald spot on Igor's head, and I suddenly understood the cause. During the course of the night, Whiskey had nurtured her son in the way she knew best. Igor had no strength to stop her, so Whiskey had licked him until there was no more hair to lick.

Knowing what I know now, if I had it to do over again, I would never have let Igor be treated with steroids. It may be rare to develop diabetes from steroids, but that was my Igor—one in a million.

Belated Gifts

TERESA OLIVE

everal years ago, our family rented a house that had a basement apartment underneath ours. The young couple who lived below us was quiet and unobtrusive. Their dog, however, was not. Cody was a typical black lab; a big, tail-thumping extrovert. He loved to greet us by planting his huge paws on our chest

Our dog, Tasha, an English Setter mix, was a kindred spirit. Since she shared the yard with Cody, they soon became fast friends. We often saw a blur of black and white fur as they raced neck and neck toward some hapless bird that had just landed in their territory.

The only time I saw any conflict between the two dogs was when we fed Tasha. Cody would bound up, expecting to share in Tasha's bounty. However, Tasha would bare her teeth and growl menacingly. Cody would change his strategy, dropping to his belly and inching slowly toward Tasha's dish. But this ingratiating behavior did not impress Tasha. The closer Cody got, the more Tasha snarled and snapped. Finally, Cody would slink away with his tail between his legs—until next mealtime, that is. Then Cody, ever the optimist, would replay the scene, with the same disappointing conclusion.

242

One day my husband, Jeff, came home visibly upset. He had just found Cody lying by the side of the road; killed by a speeding truck. Tasha sniffed at Cody's glossy black fur and whined.

Over the next few weeks, Tasha was listless; her tail drooping. She obviously missed her old friend. At the same time Tasha's food dish disappeared. We replaced it with another, only to have that one vanish as well. There followed a steady succession of bowls, aluminum plates, even an old coffee can. They all disappeared.

Finally, the mystery was solved when our neighbor knocked on our door, her arms loaded with the missing dishes, some still half-full of dog food. "Are these yours?" she asked.

When Jeff and I nodded, she explained, "I saw Tasha headed toward the road, so I shooed her back. Then I noticed all these dishes in a pile."

Puzzled, I asked, "Where were they?"

"Well, you know," she answered thoughtfully, "it was right by the place where Cody died. Isn't that odd? Surely Tasha couldn't...." Her voice trailed off in confusion.

Jeff and I exchanged glances. Could Tasha have been enticing her old friend back by offering him the one thing she withheld from him when he was alive?

Even today, retelling the story gives me chill bumps. It raises questions about animals' intelligence and emotions. It also reminds me not to wait to show love to those around me. I need to share whatever blessings I've received with others—before it's too late.

Rescuing Baxter

SUE HERSOM

t's 9 P.M., and I'm sitting in an emergency veterinary hospital waiting room. I've called my daughter to join me, and I'm desperately trying to distract myself from thinking about the condition of the 4-week-old kitten I just rescued from a schoolyard. The kitten wasn't breathing very well, and its eyes were swollen 3 times their size, literally bulging out of its head with caked mucous. I immediately rushed the baby to the emergency vet clinic, and they've taken the kitten in back. Now comes the hardest part: I have to sit and wait.

I've rescued and fostered cats for Nike Animal Rescue Foundation for fifteen years. The majority of my foster cats have been the unwanted, the discarded, the strays. All these beautiful creatures need is a little time and love. I relish loving and feeding them, kissing their soft faces and hearing their grateful, soothing purrs. In more serious cases, I've fostered cats with broken legs and emaciated bodies, but nothing prepared me for the condition of this little one.

Why do I continue to accept this sometimes gut-wrenching work that I do? My emotions can instantaneously become a roller coaster, and my heart can become heavy at any moment; yet, this experience over the years has deeply enriched my life. It fulfills me. It completes me. It has also taught my children compassion and respect for all living things. My daughter finally arrives, and I welcome the distraction from my thoughts.

The emergency room is very busy tonight. Two dogs have been hit by cars, and since the kitten is breathing okay for now, the vet is working on both of the dogs. The kitten is my priority, but I understand it is not the vet's for the moment. About an hour later, the tech comes out to tell me they need to keep him (it's a boy!) overnight in an incubator because of his low body temperature, and they will give him fluids and antibiotics. They will try to clean his eyes the best they can, but they are not very hopeful that the eyes can be saved. They tell me I can pick up the kitten tomorrow morning and bring him to our regular vet the next day. I leave the hospital with mixed emotions

I pick up the kitten early the next morning and bring him to my animal organization's vet hospital. They will do what they can to help him, but there is only a shred of hope they can save his eyes. Jenette, who is caring for him at the vet, names him "Baxter." She has volunteered to bottle-feed him during the night for the next couple of nights. I call my organization for support and guidance about what to do next. Then I make an appointment for Baxter to see an eye specialist.

A few days later, I'm sobbing as I leave his eye doctor appointment. The kitten's eyes will have to be removed when he's about 3 months old. Both his corneas are punctured. I've convinced myself he could at least see shadows, so the diagnosis crushes me. This condition could have started with an infection in the womb or even before his eyes opened after he was born. We'll never know. It doesn't matter now. He will never see. Baxter is blind.

As I dangle my fingers in front of his distorted little face, softly touching his whiskers to let him know they are there, his paws ferociously play with my fingers. Through my tears, I can't help but smile. He doesn't know. Baxter doesn't know he cannot see. He's very contented lying next to me doing what kittens do. It's my heart that is breaking.

I pick him up and put my face in front of his, and his paws immediately reach out to find it—touching it, exploring it. His whiskers brush up against my eyes, and his mouth lightly bites my nose. Purring contentedly, he rubs the right side of his head against my cheek, and the crustiness of what's left of his eye scrapes my face. He turns his face back to mine. I swear he's looking right at me. How can it be that he cannot see me?

As we rescue these animals, sometimes there are hard and difficult decisions to make. When a situation with a cat does not go as I would hope, I can still take comfort and find peace in the fact that as long as I have done all I can do, I can accept whatever is the destiny of these innocent creatures that touch my life. This is the only way I can stay balanced and sane. It's time to ask myself if Baxter should go through life without his sight. He's only 4 weeks old. There is not only a chance of infection before his surgery to think about, but also the risks of anesthesia on a kitten so young. How much do we want to put him through? With all things considered, how important is sight to a cat? I question what right do I have to make life-and-death decisions for these innocent creatures. I feel as if I'm playing God, and it's not a comfortable feeling.

I explore his precious, misshapen face, looking for answers. He purrs immediately upon my touch; he lives to play; and he's a porker when it comes to food. He is also strong and a fighter. The answer is clear. There is no decision to be made here. Of course, Baxter's life is worth saving! His life will never be "normal," but it will be Baxter's world as only he will know it.

As we foster these innocent creatures, we also need to pray for the power to let go when the time comes to say goodbye as they go to their new adoptive homes. It's difficult because these special cats become a part of our homes, our routines, our lives. When it's time for one of my foster cats to move on, I say a quiet prayer that keeps me centered and focused: "Remind me, Lord, that there's always another kitty out there to take this little one's place."

I bring Baxter back to the vet once again. Jenette is now going to take over as his foster mom. I work full-time, but she can be with him all day and night until he's old enough for his surgery. When the time comes, we'll find him just the right home for his special needs. For now, it's time for me to say goodbye, the dreadful, inevitable "letting go." I'm going to miss his dependence upon me and the way he cocks his little head when he hears my voice. My heart breaks one last time as I softly say, "I love you, Baxie," and wish him well on his journey. As I turn to leave him behind, through my tears I can barely whisper the words, "There's always another kitty out there to take this little one's place."

The Summer of the Ham Sandwiches

DIANE M. CIARLONI

don't remember how old I was before I realized a beagle wasn't the only breed of dog in the world. As far as I was concerned, he provided more than enough variety. After all, he was available in black-and-tan, black-and-white, tan-and-white, and black-tan-white. Not only did he offer a color selection, but there was also a choice of sizes: 10-inch, 12-inch, 14-inch. What more could a person want?

Beagles are also extremely smart. Well, actually, wily might be a better word. Or, better yet, a combination of wily and smart. Their primary negative factor is that hound-dog bay that can drive a person crazy. Nose pointed skyward, mouth forming a tiny Cheerio-like circle and a mournful sound coming from the throat. Sometimes so much energy is expended that the front feet actually raise off the ground slightly. Of course, there are times when beagles don't bay just for the fun of baying. Sometimes they do it because it's part of their job. Consider, as a wonderful example, Duke.

Duke was a 12-inch beagle who knew how to do just about everything. I didn't believe in harming so much as one hair on any kind of animal. My brother, on the other hand, fancied himself a rabbit hunter.

He was 16 or 17 at the time, which means I was somewhere in the vicinity of six. Now what could go better with a would-be rabbit hunter than a sure-nuff rabbit dog? Nothing. It was as natural a combination as ham 'n eggs or peas 'n carrots.

Very early one morning Fred took the 410 shotgun from the house and whistled for Duke. The duo headed for the woods behind our farm. Deciding to follow, I jumped out of bed and pulled on clothes. Once outside, I kept a respectful distance between myself and them. We passed into the woods and, almost immediately, Duke's nose went up. I'd never seen it wiggle quite so fast but, then, I'd never been rabbit hunting with him. My brother did whatever it is you do to have the gun ready to fire. Duke, looking for all the world like a person on a mission, moved solo deeper into the woods. No more than two or three minutes separated his departure and the beginning of a bay. My brother apparently knew this routine because he hefted the gun to his shoulder as soon as he heard the sound and, momentarily, a cottontail cannon-balled from the woods with Duke in hot pursuit. The beagle directed the rabbit smack in front of my brother.

Bam! The gun discharged. Bam! It discharged again. I was terrified for the rabbit but, when I looked, he was skittering back into the woods. Duke went in after him while my brother reloaded.

In no time at all Duke settled into another bay. The scene repeated itself. My brother lifted the gun. The rabbit came from the woods. Duke shoved him toward my brother. Bam! Bam! The rabbit charged back into the woods. And it happened a third time. Baying. Beagle and rabbit out of the woods. Bam! Bam! Rabbit back into the woods but, right there, the repetition stopped. Instead of returning to the woods after the rabbit, Duke turned and looked up at my brother. I'm sure he would have shaken his head if he'd known how but, instead, he turned on his heels and set out for home. In other words, enough was enough.

My father didn't believe in having animals in the house, so Duke had a huge fenced-in pen in the backyard. Of course, we lived on a farm so it wasn't really a yard, since having a backyard was nothing less than a waste of productive land. Anyway, there was a large house in Duke's pen. It was kept well-stocked with discarded blankets which, as soon as the weather turned warm, Duke promptly hauled from the house onto the front porch Daddy had built for him.

The wire surrounding the beagle's pen was made of three-inch open squares, more than large enough for Duke's paws. That dog learned how to scramble to the top of his house, and then use the roof as a launching pad to propel himself to the fence. He landed with all four legs spread and immediately hooked his front paws through two of the holes. Then, with that support, he inserted his back paws into two lower holes. It was perfect. He could then scale the fence with greater ease than the most experienced mountain climber or agile trapeze artist. He reached the top, went over and somehow managed to "walk" down the other side until he was within comfortable jumping distance. He was then free to go about his beagle business.

As soon as we realized Duke's escape technique, we took measures to prevent it by installing a board at the top of the fence and all the way around the pen. Now the enclosure looked like Alcatraz. And, now, Duke still fought his way to freedom.

The beagle escaped nearly every night. He didn't go anywhere other than the screened door to the screened porch attached to the back of our house. Again, using his multi-talented paws, he opened the door and entered. The first thing he did was check Mama's old wringer-style washing machine. She sometimes put clothes in there in the evening, intending to wash them the next morning. If that were the case, Duke jumped in and made a comfortable bed. If not, he helped himself to the ratty sofa that provided Daddy a place to sit while he shed his dirty work shoes before going into the house. I don't think the washing machine or the sofa were any more comfortable than the pile of blankets in his house. I just think he wanted to be closer to his family in case we needed him during the dark.

There was a large factory across the road from our house. It was originally built during World War II to produce munitions. I don't really remember what it did when I was a kid, but I do remember there were lots of workers.

Duke disappeared for a while every day but there was nothing alarming about that. You see, Duke was a confident beagle. He knew his way around the area. He knew how to hunt on his own (he certainly couldn't depend on my brother) and he knew how to escape his pen. His personality and demeanor were—well—a bit on the strange side. Truthfully, I think it was because he considered himself to be far more human than canine.

Everyone in the immediate region knew Duke. Many knew him by name and others by sight. It was a good thing because the beagle harbored one extremely bad habit. That is, he didn't believe in walking along the side of the road. No. Instead, he walked smack down the middle. Many times we saw cars stop for him or move to the opposite side of the road to accommodate his passage. Try as we might, we couldn't teach him differently.

Anyway, back to the factory and the wily beagle's daily disappearances. His absences didn't really settle on our conscious awareness level unless we happened to call him and he didn't answer. Otherwise, he was just gone until, one day, his timing and mine happened to coincide. I was outside and, just as I looked up, Duke was turning into the driveway. That was fine, but there was something dangling from his mouth. It was…it was…a brown paper lunch bag. I removed it from his mouth (he didn't protest) and opened it. There was a piece of cake and two ham sandwiches.

250

"Duke, where in the...," before I finished the question, a fellow in work coveralls came striding down the driveway, calling "Hey! Hey! Is that your dog?" Oh, no.

"Yes, sir," I answered. Duke turned, positioned himself next to me, and sat against my legs.

I was definitely relieved when the man's mouth turned into a smile, a very small smile but still a smile. "He's been coming over to the factory for about a month now and stealing lunches. Sometimes he steals one, eats it on the spot and then steals another one to take with him."

"But how does he get to them?" I asked. "Where do you leave them?"

"We have a small coatroom," he explained, "before you go into the main part of the factory. We leave our lunches there."

"How do you get into the room from the outside?" I asked. I felt as if I were reconstructing the scene of a crime.

"A screen door," he said.

The mystery was solved. There wasn't a screen door within 500 miles that Duke couldn't handle.

"Did you look to see what kind of sandwich was in the bag?"

"Ham." He started laughing. "He never steals the bags with bologna in them. It's always the ham."

I held out the rescued bag. "Would you like to take this back to"... I looked at the name written in the outside..."Sam?" Without waiting for an answer, I said "I can try really hard to keep him at home."

The man shook his head. "Sam needs to take off a few pounds, so let the beagle keep the sandwich. As far as keeping him home, well, we're kind of used to seeing him. We'd probably miss him." Actually, Duke needed the same thing as Sam. Six weeks of ham sandwiches had added a few pounds to his 12-inch frame.

It was Duke's bad habit of walking down the middle of the road that took him from us. He was six years old. It was a summer afternoon. He was returning from a visit to my cousin's house. And he was, of course, walking down the middle of the road. He was no more than a matter of feet from turning into the driveway when a car seemed to come from the proverbial nowhere. Duke didn't stand a chance. I was in the front yard with a baseball bat, watching the faithful beagle who thought he was a person make his way to his family. I saw the car hit

251

him and I knew he was dead and, for the first time in my young life, I experienced two emotions. The first was gut-wrenching grief and the second was equally gut-wrenching rage.

There was no way the driver of the car couldn't have known what happened. Yet he never slowed down. Brandishing my baseball bat over my head, I began running down the road as fast as my legs would carry me. "Come back here!" I screamed. "You killed my dog." I ran until my legs were collapsing...until I could no longer see the green car...until I felt my brother grab me from the back and carry me home.

It was amazing how many people came by during the next week and offered their condolences. It was amazing because ours was a farming community and such grief over a dog wasn't 100-percent seemly. Then one day a group of coverall-clad guys from the factory knocked on our door. One handed me a brown paper bag. Inside was a picture of Duke. One of the men had captured him on film with a hefty ham sandwich hanging from his mouth. They'd blown it up and put it in a frame. I looked up to thank them but the leader held up his hand.

"He was a good beagle," he said. "We'd give up all our lunches to have him back."

Yeah. He was a good beagle. I wasn't 10-years-old yet, but I knew that surviving this grief meant I'd be able to survive anything life sent my way. Not because I was so strong. Oh, no, not at all. But, rather, because Duke would be right there to remind me of the "summer of the ham sandwiches."

Connections

DR. JANICE K. WIESEN

he houses on our street were wrapped in sleep. Not even the sound of a passing car could be heard. Then, as had happened so many nights before, I once again was awakened by the plaintive sounds of muffled barks and moans.

As if a magnet were pulling me from my bed, I headed to the door of my bedroom, opened it and, holding tremulously to the banister, descended the steps to the second floor.

"Mom, did you hear it too? Just like the other nights." There on the landing stood my son, Brad, outside his bedroom door. He already had switched on the hall light.

The mournful wailing suddenly came to an end. Brad and I stood transfixed.

"Mom, that was Caesar! Wasn't it?"

I had to agree, even though the entire happening seemed so far-fetched. Caesar, our male basset hound, had passed away just recently. In his prime he could often be seen in a comfortable reclining position at the top of the landing, his massive jowls flopping over his front paws, to be topped only by his pendulous ears, which I always joked could easily have been tied in a bow around his rich amber-colored, silken head.

To my knowledge there can be nothing more appealing, more pathetic, than the face of a male basset with his sunken eyes. To me, that conjured up a scenario of his just having been thrown out of the nearest pub. What a sad sack! But that Dufus had the most loving, person-hugging appeal. That is, after our soul connection had been made.

Caesar had been found as my dad drove on an upstate highway. This wraith seemed to come out of nowhere. The first glance highlighted a bag of ribs and the grime of centuries on his weak frame. He offered no challenge to my father's extended hands and allowed himself to be carried. Once in the car and settled in the back seat, the wails began. The entire journey was accompanied by this uncomfortable, ghostly wailing, stopping only when he exited the car and my father introduced him to us. "Since you already have a female basset, I thought you would be pleased to accept a male," my dad explained.

What a contrast to our female, who was pleasingly well rounded, meticulously groomed and enjoying any and every lounging facility in the house. Royalty showed. What topsy turvy shenanigans would we be in for now? This Hound of the Baskervilles had really come out of the moors, and little did I know how he would turn my life around.

The first salient manner of action was to offer him some food, which he unhesitatingly accepted. Then we got him back in the car and off to the vet. But I had not anticipated the devil's soliloquy that began as soon as the car moved. What an outburst of pathos, with combinations of wails and moans! But we did forge ahead. With the veterinarian's support, eventually this mammoth, from who knows where, had a covering of a smooth white coat over his rickety ribs. That allowed his ebony markings to shimmer.

So now we had two tri-colored bassets. Since we already had Cleopatra, it was obvious the male would be called Caesar. Anthony seemed too ordinary.

There was nothing ordinary about Caesar. He was a first-class opera singer, and very ungrudgingly assisted the community's fire alarms every time they sounded. He needed no invitation. He had true community spirit.

As massive as he was compared to Cleo, he was subservient to her demands. And she made them. One bark from her and he was frozen in space. But the camaraderie between them was beautiful. We all took walks together; they ate together and slept side by side, sometimes in their special beds, but mostly both on my feet in my bed. Playing tug-of-war with old socks was a favorite pastime. And the most fun of all, for me, was dressing them up to take them to my elementary school classes for special occasions. The children loved their St. Patty's Day outfits. Brad and I even bought them ponchos and sombreros from Mexico for El Cinco de Mayo. And Cleo had a lovely black lace mantilla and fan we brought back from Madrid. Both dogs were amenable to being primped.

But the dearest recollection of Caesar is his paternal interest in the birth of our kittens. (We also had a cat, a gorgeous champagne-tangerine Angora.) Caesar stood guard over the special birthing carton we had prepared for the occasion. He observed the entire procedure and became surrogate father, not only inside the house, but also when the kittens were old enough to be in the garden. He guarded them continually, even allowing Mama Cat to go for a walk or take a nap. Caesar kept the babes from straying, always rounding them up and back to the starting point. Cleo, for the most part, was an observer, although she did sniff the kitties and even took naps with them.

We were grateful for the additions to our menagerie. And we did have a menagerie. The heart of our home also had room for twenty-six land tortoises, which were housed in a nature preserve in our garden. The dogs had no inhibitions about joining them as they ate. In fact, whether outdoors or inside, it was not unusual to see the dogs, the felines and the turtles all together on the grass or on the floor. There was no separation of species or breed. None of the animals knew what they were. They just were! And we were all family.

The kittens grew and were adopted by loving hands. Mama cat, Tobrina, now had time to lounge whenever and wherever. She had earned her rest. She had left her mark on posterity. Now her days would all be hers and hers alone.

Caesar, unfortunately, even with his comforts over the years, never fully recouped his health. Where he had come from, what his early years had been, his fearful fixation when riding in a car, all were unknown entities. The only determination at the very beginning was that he was covered with fleas and ticks and bugged by arthritis. No wonder! When my dad found him, it was in a pouring rain and he was drenched. How many days, weeks, or months had he been an outcast in all kinds of weather? Now his problems increased and he was only about six years old. A multitude of tests and treatments ensued. His urinary problem had me walking the streets every two hours during the night. He finally began to really ail. It was suggested I take him for exploratory surgery to check the adrenal glands. I could not do that to such a sweet soul. We held on as long as we could to keep him from suffering, and then the decision had to be made.

For weeks Cleo searched the house, seemed melancholy, slept less with me, but more in his bed. Life for her had changed, as it had for us all. Even Tobrina kept sniffing his bed.

And now Brad and I faced each other on the landing night after night, having been drawn to Caesar's looking-down post. We had been summoned to this spot. Had he summoned us? Had we imagined it? If so, how could both Brad and I meet at the same time? Wouldn't our imaginations have been different and at different times? How many more nights would we be meeting on the landing? Was our darling Caesar still in pain or just checking in to say he was still part of the family?

Curious unanswered questions. And more persisted. Months later I was away from home on a six-week trip to the Soviet Union. When I returned, I noticed that Cleo had difficulty walking up the steps. A visit to the vet showed a disk problem. As anyone knows, a basset hound is half a dog high and three dogs long, so you can imagine the extend of her back problem.

To ease her situation, I opted to sleep down in the den with her so she would be on level ground and also have access to the backyard. That helped somewhat, but she continued to show discomfort. Another trip to the vet and I was told to check her into the hospital. The day I was to bring her back home, the doctor was handing me some special medication, and as I held Cleo's leash in my hand she suddenly became violently ill. The doctor said that if I took her home I'd be back in a few hours. He tried to ease my shocked realization that this was it.

I left the hospital in a veil of tears, barely able to find my car. When I did it was there I sat for at least an hour before wending my way home.

Once home, I immediately called my very dear cousin, Laurie, who had gone through this several times with her pets. She understood my agony. As we spoke, I looked out of the front window as my doorbell began to ring. My mother went to the back door to see if anyone was there. Once again, no one! Yet the bell continued to ring and ring and then finally stopped.

My cousin said, "Don't you know what that was all about?"

"No, I haven't any idea," I answered. "It's just so strange."

"Honey, it's Cleo. She's leaving us and wants you to know."

"Oh! My God!" I gasped.

Loving connections we make in life do spill over. They always remain a part of us. Just because our pets are a different breed from us does not mean they have not made connections, soulful connections, to us. The answers will remain a mystery, but I'd feel comforted to know that Cleo and Caesar, in their very own way, sealed a bond with us forever.

Now every time I hear the fire alarms, I'll hear Caesar. Every time I see a large bar of baking chocolate, I'll recall the day Caesar managed to open the kitchen cabinet and proceed to devour the entire bar along with the wrapping. What a week that was!

And with Cleo, each time I hear the raucous blue jay, I'll feel her presence, remembering how she accompanied him with her bark as the jay continued his song.

Then there were those bath sessions with the hounds. I carried them up the steps into the tub, only to have them jump out as soon as they thought they were "salon-ed" enough. Then the two of them ran up and down the steps, shaking their heads, flapping their ears, flipping every extra remnant of the EVENT far away.

At that point in time it was no holds barred. Only THEIR traffic was allowed. Every place was theirs, especially the beds. It seemed to be a marathon between the two of them, finding extra places to pounce upon. Exhausting though it was for me, as I tried to keep out of their hectic paths, I'd do it all over again.

These subtle connections of the heart—what they are, how they start—can only be imagined. Did we imagine Caesar on the landing? Did we imagine Cleo ringing the bell? Who can tell?

Memorial Services

JOE McCABE

hroughout the late 1980's and all of the 1990's, my wife, Hilda, and I lived on a farm in West Virginia. Our yard was approximately one-and-a-half acres and was bordered on all sides by meadows. A farmer rented the meadows, and he put a herd of cattle there to graze. He had four bulls and more than a hundred cows in his herd. Every spring almost every cow would produce one or two calves.

Hilda and I had a large organic garden, and we enjoyed working surrounded by the cows. Frequently, a cow would find a way through the three-strand barbed-wire fence that separated our yard from the meadows, so we became adept at herding cows to and through the gate that led from our yard into the east meadow.

One day during the spring calving season we heard many cows calling in distress in the east meadow. A group of them were milling around on an upward sloping section several hundred yards from our gate. Eventually, the cows moved north, and we noticed a large dark object on the ground where they had been. Hilda and I entered the meadow to investigate. As we drew closer, we realized that it was a cow lying on her side with her legs pointing uphill.

When we reached her, we saw that a calf was half out of her birth canal. Both the cow and the calf were dead. The mother had been trying to give birth uphill and had failed. This must have been her first calf. She was too inexperienced to know that giving birth downhill would have been easy, but giving birth uphill was impossible. None of her sisters had been able to turn her over and save her life.

We went home and phoned the bad news to the farmer. He sent one of his sons to check on the cow that day, but it took him several days to get a truck with a hoist to remove the bodies from the meadow.

That afternoon, around four-thirty, the biggest bull in the herd stood near the dead cow and called loudly. Soon the whole herd assembled from all over the meadows; the other bulls and all the cows came and gathered around the dead mother and her calf.

Hilda and I watched with amazement. For nearly half an hour the whole herd stood facing the dead. Some of them made low sounds. No church congregation could have been more reverent than these cows were. Eventually, they all wandered off to munch the grass of the meadow.

Hilda and I decided that we had witnessed a memorial service conducted by cows. We had never seen anything like it before.

The following morning, around eleven, we heard the big red bull calling again. And we watched as the whole herd again gathered as before, for approximately half an hour. That afternoon, again around four-thirty, the bull called the herd together. Every day at eleven and four-thirty the bull summoned them, and they came and stayed for half an hour.

After the truck came and removed the bodies from the meadow, the herd continued to assemble twice a day, everyday, at the same place and times. This went on for nearly three weeks.

One afternoon Hilda and I realized that the cows had not conducted a memorial service that morning. There was none that afternoon. Nor ever again.

That was the only cow who died in the meadows while we lived on the farm. We were sorry for her and her calf and for the farmer, but we were grateful that we had been able to observe the memorial services the cows conducted for their sister and her calf. These services were in their way as wonderful and mysterious as any we ever attended for our dear, departed human friends and relatives.

A Note from the Editors

This original book was created by the Books and Inspirational Media Division of Guideposts, the world's leading inspirational publisher. Founded in 1945 by Dr. Norman Vincent Peale and Ruth Stafford Peale, Guideposts helps people from all walks of life achieve their maximum personal and spiritual potential. Guideposts is committed to communicating positive, faith-filled principles for people everywhere to use in successful daily living.

Our publications include award-winning magazines such as *Guideposts* and *Angels on Earth,* best-selling books, and outreach services that demonstrate what can happen when faith and positive thinking are applied in day-to-day life.

For more information, visit us at www.guideposts.com, call (800) 932-2145 or write Guideposts, PO Box 5815, Harlan, Iowa 51593.